THE CANCER DIET
COOKBOOK FOR BEGINNERS

The Complete Cancer Diet Guide With Essential Nourishing Whole-Food

Anticancer Recipes For Treatment And Recovery| With 28-Day Meal Plan|

With Premium Full Color Pictures

DINA S. ROY

Table of Contents

Introduction

People call me Dina, but my full name is Dina S. Roy. Honestly, I love my life. My mantra was "You Only Live Once," which motivated me to cross every boundary. I mean, who doesn't deserve to enjoy the world to the fullest?

But soon, my world began to crash right before my eyes – or, maybe, so I thought. It started with constant itching in my nipple area, and I thought it was just a minor infection. I took an antibiotic and thought that should work.

Sadly, a few weeks after taking the antibiotic, the itching returned. This time, there was scaling, peeling, and flaking of the pigmented part of my breast skin; I had to visit the doctor for a proper diagnosis.

I was utterly shocked when the numerous tests and scans revealed I had breast cancer.

My doctor was excellent. He helped me a lot. Fixing multiple appointments and connecting me with a support group were actions that gave me another shot at life. I overcame cancer; these people guided me through good dieting, adequate treatment, positive affirmations, exercises, breaking bad habits, and cultivating good living habits.

Although this book is centered on healthy foods and cooking strategies that could help your cancer recovery journey, I have dedicated this introduction to comprehensively exploring actions and decisions, cutting across proper treatment, joining support groups, good dieting, etc., that contributed to my victorious emergence from breast cancer.

Chapter 1
Basics of Cancer

Proper Treatment

Getting proper treatment was my major priority, beyond the other actions and activities I engaged in. Cancer treatments could be administered based on your doctor's suggestions and your agreement. For me, the doctor recommended combining immunotherapy, hormonal therapy, and hyperthermia.

Of course, beyond these recommendations, there are a few more cancer treatment methods, including:

1. Surgery: This cancer treatment involves cutting out the cancerous cells and the affected surrounding tissues to stop the further growth of the cancerous cells. Best for solid tumors, surgery can be combined with chemotherapy or radiation.
2. Chemotherapy: Chemotherapy is the usage of drugs to destroy cancerous cells. These drugs can be administered orally or through blood vessels. Like surgery, Chemo can also be combined with other treatment methods.
3. Radiation Therapy: Radiation therapy is also called radiotherapy. It uses intense radiation to kill or shrink cancerous cells through X-rays or radioactive seeds to damage their DNA.
4. Targeted Therapies: This method involves using drugs to target cancer cells and proteins that aid the growth, multiplication, and spread of these cancerous cells.
5. Immunotherapy: Immunotherapy leverages the body's ability to counter infections. Substances produced by the body or in the lab are used to solidify the immune system's effectiveness in fighting cancer.
6. Hormonal Therapy: Hormonal Therapy involves using medications to prevent the number of particular hormones in the body that supports the growth of cancerous cells. It can be administered through pills, capsules, syrups, implants, injections, or surgery. Although effective, Hormonal Therapy has its accompanying side effects.
7. Hyperthermia: Hyperthermia involves heating the body tissue to as high as 113°F, damaging and killing cancerous cells. Hyperthermia can be used to treat appendix cancer, brain cancer, breast cancer, and cervical cancer among others.
8. Laser Therapy: Laser Therapy uses a thin, focused light beam to destroy and kill cancerous cells. The laser types used for treating cancer include carbon dioxide lasers, neodymium, yttrium-aluminum-garnet lasers, and argon lasers.
9. Photodynamic Therapy: It uses light-activated drugs, a photosensitizing agent, to destroy or kill cancerous cells. Exposing cancerous cells that have absorbed the photosensitizing agent to a specific light wavelength causes the photosensitizer to produce oxygen radicals that kill the cancerous cells.
10. Cryotherapy: Cryosurgery uses extreme cold generated through liquid nitrogen to destroy cancerous cells.
11. Clinical Trials: This is another treatment option for some people and has resulted in new discoveries in the medical world. It involves performing live trials of clinically tested medications.

Clinical Trials

Clinical trials aim to develop better treatments and explore various ways of preventing, diagnosing, and treating cancer.

Because of the skepticism surrounding clinical trials, I will discuss a few of its benefits.

If you are recently diagnosed with cancer, you might opt for the clinical trial treatment over others for various

reasons, including a tight budget, unresponsiveness to the previous treatments, etc.

Most doctors recommend clinical trials to their patients irrespective of their cancer type or stage because of the associated benefits – but, of course, they do not force it on you.

TOP 4 BENEFITS OF CLINICAL TRIALS

1. Access to The Latest Therapies:

Clinical trials allow you to access new and recent cancer treatment innovations.

The world is evolving, and new discoveries are made daily. These latest discoveries could help you avoid experiencing certain side effects associated with other cancer treatment methods like chemotherapy, immunotherapy, etc.

2. Closer monitoring

Patients undergoing clinical trials are typically more closely observed for side effects, reactions, and progress than other treatment methods.
Aside from the closer monitoring, the population for a clinical trial is lower compared to a regular hospital. Thus, doctors can attend to everyone effectively and on a more personal level.

Many cancer patients sometimes believe they will be treated as "guinea pigs," which is not true. You have the benefit of getting extra care from a team of doctors and nurses available to address your questions and uncertainties.

3. Reduced Cost

Usually, patients are not responsible for their medications and treatments during a clinical trial because they are covered by the sponsors of the research or government. Nevertheless, they might be responsible for some expenses like travel and imaging services, which the research does not cover.

Whether fully sponsored or not, you can be sure that it would be a reduced cost compared to personally paying for the whole treatment.

4. It Promotes A Sense of Fulfilment

If everyone avoids clinical trials, the researchers will not be able to introduce new and better treatments into the medical field. Persons who participate in clinical trials and confirm the effectiveness of a proposed cancer treatment or medication can gain a sense of fulfillment, having contributed to something life-transforming.

Good Faith and Affirmations

Every time I stood from my bed, I reminded myself that it was another day to go harder, fight fiercer, and believe more. I attended treatment sessions with high expectations, assessing my body whenever I could to track my health improvement.

Aside from the physical and biological effects, cancer can also be psychologically and mentally damaging. Therefore, you must constantly remind yourself of what lies beyond the cancer hurdle. You owe this to yourself.

You need to remind yourself that your cancer doesn't define you. Attend events that will lighten your mood.

Although there is no scientific proof that having a positive attitude cures cancer, maintaining negativity, at best, denies you the opportunity to use your time and life judiciously. You must constantly remind yourself that your life matters, and you shouldn't entirely put it on hold due to cancer.

Undeniably, treating cancer can be a lot: you may need to suspend several lifestyles and activities to focus on your health and quick recovery. Nevertheless, there are several other things you can engage in that will give you a new reason to smile and enjoy your wonderful life.

TOP REASONS YOU SHOULD MAKE POSITIVE AFFIRMATIONS

1. Maintains your hope for survival: Making positive affirmations boosts your confidence that you will survive and fully recover. Sometimes I didn't want to continue because I wasn't noticing any progress. However, my

positive affirmation kept me alert and reminded me that another therapy would move me closer to complete recovery.

2. Help you radiate good energy: Positive affirmations keep you in a good mood. It helps you smile, laugh, and talk more. These habits generally brighten the mood of others around you.

3. Reduces your chances of depression: Many cancer patients get depressed; unfortunately, it can kill them even faster than cancerous cells.

4. You will enjoy life regardless of your health status: positive affirmations help cancer patients have a fulfilled life despite their condition. I didn't imagine myself writing a cancer diet cookbook before I had cancer. Still, I am grateful for how far I've come and the opportunity to guide others through their cancer-fighting journey through healthy eating.

5. It Challenges the Conventional After-Cancer Trauma: Positive affirmations make it possible for cancer patients to avoid experiencing the traumatic after-effect of cancer treatment.

Support Groups

A week after I commenced my treatment, my doctor recommended that I join a support group. Honestly, I didn't know what to expect – I had never been to one before. However, my principal motivation for attending was the understanding that I couldn't do it alone.

My first time with the support group was memorable; I don't see myself forgetting that experience anytime soon. They warmly welcomed me as though I was their long-lost family. I never expected such a stigma-free society. It was great, and I immediately felt hope and a reason to smile again, alongside accelerated confidence for survival.

Trust me, every cancer patient needs a support system, whether in the form of family, friends, or support groups and if possible, you can have them all.

TOP REASONS TO BE BART OF A SUPPORT GROUP

1. They are more informed: There are various support groups, including peer, professional, and informational support groups. However, all the different support groups have one thing in common: information and knowledge. They offer a different perspective as they speak and share from personal experiences.

2. They create a home outside the home: Support groups are an excellent place to call home, especially for patients that don't have anyone to care for them. Most cancer patients' primary reason for depression is isolation, whether self-inflicted or circumstance-created. Although members of your support groups won't always be with you, the understanding that you aren't the only warrior and that you are loved and wanted by certain people puts you at peace.

3. Freedom of expression: Many cancer patients don't feel comfortable expressing themselves to others because they believe they cannot understand, irrespective of how much they explain. Support groups won't force you to say what you don't want to say. You're allowed to share your stories when and how you like.

4. You can learn from others' experiences: You can learn from what others did, avoided, and what was beneficial to their recovery. However, whatever you learn, always cross-check with your doctor to know if its applicable to you.

5. You get to establish new networks: Life and purpose are hinged on beneficial networking. Beyond learning from the experience of others and also building my confidence, I made new friends and created connections that are still strong to date.

6. Support groups help eliminate loneliness: Battling cancer can be very lonely. People have their breaking points, which is understandable. But belonging to a dedicated support group can help eliminate any possibility of feeling lonely. There, you are amongst people who share the same burden as you and understand how you may feel. In addition, it increases a community feeling that helps you know you are not in it alone.

Chapter 2
Start your Cancer Diet Journey

Good Dieting

Good dieting contributed significantly to my cancer recovery. I began to eat food not because I was hungry but because I was intentional about building a solid immune system.

A healthy diet maintains and contributes to an individual's overall health. It ensures that the body is not malnourished and is equipped with all the nutrients necessary to fight against germs and diseases. Essential nutrients the body needs to build the immune system include fluid, proteins, vitamins, fiber, fruits, whole grains, vegetables, low-fat milk, etc.

TOP BENEFITS OF HEALTHY DIETING WHILE FIGHTING CANCER

1. Increases your strength and energy: It's typical for cancer-fighting warriors to find it challenging when engaging in certain activities. And this is because cancer is strength-draining; to regain lost strength and energy, you need to eat well.
2. Reduces the risk of infection: Healthy dieting helps build your immune system, reducing the risks of infection. The body requires specific nutritional content to develop the immune system to fight against infection and diseases.
3. Manage the side effects of cancer treatments: Cancer treatment has many accompanying side effects like nausea, hair loss, loss of appetite, etc. Healthy dieting helps reduce most of these side effects to a considerable extent.
4. It helps you to sleep better: A healthy diet consists of the 6 major classes of food that helps cancer patients sleep better and reduce cancer after-effects.
5. Retains body weight: Some side effects of cancer treatments, like vomiting, eliminate body fluid. Simultaneously, loss of appetite prevents the body from getting the required nutrients to regain lost body resources, which results in weight loss. However, healthy dieting helps you to retain and build your weight. Please note that healthy dieting doesn't imply quantity eating; instead, it means providing your body with the required nutrients for effective functioning.
6. Hastens recovery and healing: Although nutritious food cannot solely cure cancer, it can facilitate healing. If your body is not fit to receive and process the treatment administered, it will negatively impact your general recovery; this is the primary reason healthy dieting is essential.

Good Living Habit

A healthy, sound, and long life is generally desirable. Therefore, practicing good living habits is not a trend; instead, it is a way of life that everyone should practice.

Cancer patients should constantly practice good living habits to ensure a seamless recovery and not complicate their overall health. The following are good living habits that will contribute to your recovery process:

1. Don't shy away from emotional support: People have differing reactions to the realization of cancer. While some are readily open to receiving emotional support from loved ones and families, others naturally shut everyone off from themselves. You need as much emotional help as possible, even if it is just from your little circle of comfort.
2. Reduce stressful activities: One of the mistakes people with health conditions tend to make is to act on the desire to prove they can still do activities they previously did before their health condition. However, trust me, you don't have to prove yourself to anyone to be you. Stressing your body beyond its present capacity will only negatively affect your health and slow your recovery.
3. Sleep adequately: Cancer patients are susceptible to a disordered sleeping pattern because of the cancerous cells, medications, treatments, depression, pain, anxiety, etc. This, in turn, affects your thinking, blood pressure, appetite, immune system, and overall health. Hence, it is necessary to get adequate sleep to help your recovery process. If you find it challenging to sleep adequately, you should visit your doctor for an assessment and get a solution for a possible sleeping disorder.
4. Eat healthily: Healthy eating is essential for quick recovery. Eat less junk and more nutritious food to ensure your body gets the required nutrients for survival.
5. Maintain a clean and pollution-free environment: Diseases and infections thrive in a dirty and polluted environment. Cleanliness and hygiene are good living habits that everyone should practice. Maintaining a clean and pollution-free environment while you are receiving treatment helps ensure you do not complicate your health condition.
6. Avoid alcohol consumption: As much as you can, avoid alcohol consumption during and after cancer treatment. Alcohol can worsen the negative impact of specific cancer treatments like chemotherapy and increase the risk of a more complicated cancer diagnosis.
7. Avoid smoking or tobacco usage: Research by the US Centre for Disease Control and Prevention has shown that smokers' bodies begin to heal 20 minutes after their last cigarette. This means cigarette or tobacco consumption slows your recovery process and can complicate your health condition even further.
8. Be happy: Many people find it difficult to be happy when their life isn't going as they intended. Regardless of the situation, try to find happiness in yourself and your loved ones.
9. Exercise: Exercising during cancer treatment is vital for developing your overall mental and physical health. However, you shouldn't partake in all kinds of workouts, depending on the nature of the cancer and the treatment method explored. Consult a fitness consultant to determine the best exercise for you.

Exercising

Exercising enhances your mental and physical health. However, consult with your doctor about your exercise plan and schedule.

IMPORTANCE OF EXERCISING DURING CANCER TREATMENT

1. It helps you sleep better: Moderate aerobic exercises increase deep sleep, allowing the brain and body to relax.
2. It strengthens your brain and your body for effective work: When you exercise, your body and your muscles stretch, which helps to enhance your brain and body functions.
3. Reduces the risk of depression and anxiety: Physical activity boosts individuals' physical and mental effectiveness. Therefore, when cancer patients exercise, it reduces depression and anxiety, which are majorly a function of our mental capacity.
4. Boosts your appetite: Ordinarily, after exercising, you have little or no hunger for food because of the rise in your body temperature. However, after cooling, you will have an increased appetite that motivates you to eat nourishing food.
5. Develops life quality: Exercise improves overall health and reduces the chances of certain infections and diseases, boosting the quality of life.
6. It reduces or stops the growth of cancer cells: Exercise reduces or prevents the growth of cancer cells by releasing myokines into your blood.
7. Reduces fatigue and tiredness: Moderate exercise improves the body's cardiovascular health and overall body fitness. It also contributes to the even circulation of oxygen, reducing constant fatigue and tiredness over time.
8. Improves self-confidence: Exercise helps you see yourself in a better light and boost your self-esteem because it gives you a better body image and strengthens your body and heart.
9. Brightens your mood: The body releases chemicals that increase an individual's overall well-being and reduce the production of chemicals that foster anxiety.
10. It Prevents lymphoedema: Lymphoedema is caused by swelling in the body tissue. Exercise helps to prevent lymphoedema because it improves the flow of lymph fluid and reduces the risk of lymphoedema.

Despite the importance of exercising during recovery, it could negatively affect your health if you engage in specific exercises without extra care and due consultation. You need to take extra care and consult a physician before engaging in exercises, if:

1. The cancerous cells affect your bones.
2. Your immunity is low.
3. You recently had surgery.
4. You are experiencing peripheral neuropathy.

TOP EXERCISES TO DO DURING AND AFTER CANCER

i. Treatment
ii. Squatting
iii. Stair climbing
iv. Swimming
v. Jogging
vi. Sweeping
vii. Dancing
viii. Walking a dog
ix. Weeding your garden
x. Bike riding
xi. Car washing.

HOW MUCH EXERCISE DO YOU NEED?

The American Cancer Society recommends a minimum of 30 to 60 minutes of exercise for the general population for a minimum of 5 days within a week. Generally, cancer patients ought to exercise gradually and not just dive into exercising to prevent further damage. The level and the nature of your exercise largely depend on your health status and your doctor's prescription.

Although cancer is not planned, it should not stop your life. You can even navigate an entirely new path despite the hurdle of cancer, just like I did to impact other people. This cookbook will expose you to various foods that are healthy for consumption by cancer patients and improve your overall health.
See you on the next page!

Week 1

Here is the following first week's meal plan for the cancer diet. Try to follow the plan thoroughly to start getting the benefits of a cancer diet.

Meal Plan	Breakfast	Lunch	Dinner	Snack
Day-1	Amazing Acai Breakfast Smoothie	Black Bean Soup	Crazy Sexy Bean Chili	Hard Vegan Cheese
Day-2	Blueberry Walnut Oatmeal	Anita Moorjani'S Coconut Curry	Aromatic Lentil Soup	Hard Vegan Cheese
Day-3	Pumpkin Overnight Oats	Raw Lasagna	Raw Lasagna	Hard Vegan Cheese
Day-4	Vegetable Cheddar Egg Muffins	Cauliflower Popcorn	Spring Green Soup	Hard Vegan Cheese
Day-5	Green Smoothie Bowl	Bean Burgers	Chicken Tortilla Soup	Chickpea Fries
Day-6	Summer Vegetable Frittata	Anita Moorjani'S Coconut Curry	Crazy Sexy Bean Chili	Chickpea Fries
Day-7	Coconut Wraps	Cauliflower Crust Mini Pizzas	Cauliflower Crust Mini Pizzas	Hummus-Stuffed Peppers

Week 2

Here is the following second week's meal plan for a cancer diet. It's the second stage of the 4 weeks meal plan that you must take into account carefully.

Meal Plan	Breakfast	Lunch	Dinner	Snack
Day-1	Blueberry Walnut Oatmeal	Hummus-Stuffed Peppers	Cauliflower Rice	Cancer'S Gone Crackers
Day-2	Pumpkin Overnight Oats	Lemony Chicken Soup	Black Bean Bowl with Sweet Potatoes and Roasted Chickpeas	Cancer'S Gone Crackers
Day-3	Stovetop Steel-Cut Oats with Banana, Cherries, and Almonds	Raw Lasagna	Emerald Greens with Orange	Cancer'S Gone Crackers
Day-4	Summer Vegetable Frittata	Lemony Chicken Soup	Raw Lasagna	Cancer'S Gone Crackers
Day-5	Amazing Acai Breakfast Smoothie	Cauliflower Rice	Hummus-Stuffed Peppers	Cancer'S Gone Crackers
Day-6	Emerald Greens with Orange	Harira-Inspired Stew	Harira-Inspired Stew	Gluten-Free Tortillas
Day-7	Emerald Greens with Orange	Emerald Greens with Orange	Black Bean Bowl with Sweet Potatoes and Roasted Chickpeas	Gluten-Free Tortillas

Week 3

Here is the following third week's meal plan for a cancer diet. In this stage, you already got the result of the previous two weeks' diet plan. So, follow this third stage of the meal plan completely to get a better result.

Meal Plan	Breakfast	Lunch	Dinner	Snack
Day-1	Open-Faced Baked Eggs	Arugula with Edamame, Radish, and Avocado	Pumpkin Curry Soup	Teff Crepes
Day-2	Tofu Breakfast Scramble	Warm Napa Cabbage Slaw	Chickpea Burgers	Teff Crepes
Day-3	Amazing Acai Breakfast Smoothie	Warm and Toasty Cumin Carrots	Emerald Greens with Orange	Teff Crepes
Day-4	Pumpkin Overnight Oats	Pumpkin Curry Soup	Warm and Toasty Cumin Carrots	Teff Crepes
Day-5	Blueberry Walnut Oatmeal	Mushroom Barley Soup	Warm Napa Cabbage Slaw	Hard Vegan Cheese
Day-6	Spiced Squash Soup	Chickpea Burgers	Arugula with Edamame, Radish, and Avocado	Hard Vegan Cheese
Day-7	Cashew Cheese	Emerald Greens with Orange	Green Beans with Brazil Nuts and Basil	Hard Vegan Cheese

Week 4

This is the final stage of our 4 week's cancer diet meal plan. In this stage, you already have formed a habit of maintaining a cancer diet. So, follow this final stage to get best the best result in your body and mind.

Meal Plan	Breakfast	Lunch	Dinner	Snack
Day-1	Amazing Acai Breakfast Smoothie	Zucchini Spaghetti With Raw Tomato Sauce And Walnut "Meatballs"	Zucchini Spaghetti With Raw Tomato Sauce And Walnut "Meatballs"	Cancer'S Gone Crackers
Day-2	Blueberry Walnut Oatmeal	Anita Moorjani'S Coconut Curry	Cauliflower Rice	Cancer'S Gone Crackers
Day-3	Baked Pears with Greek Yogurt	Aromatic Lentil Soup	Aromatic Lentil Soup	Gluten-Free Tortillas
Day-4	Open-Faced Baked Eggs	Kale with Carrots	Zucchini Pasta with Broccoli Sprouts Pesto	Gluten-Free Tortillas
Day-5	Amazing Acai Breakfast Smoothie	Mashed Cinnamon Butternut Squash	Anita Moorjani'S Coconut Curry	Coconut Wraps
Day-6	Pumpkin Overnight Oats	Zucchini Pasta with Broccoli Sprouts Pesto	Zucchini Pasta with Broccoli Sprouts Pesto	Coconut Wraps
Day-7	Open-Faced Baked Eggs	Cauliflower Crust Mini Pizzas	Spring Green Soup	Guacamole

Pumpkin Overnight Oats

Prep time: 5 minutes | Rest time: 15 minutes, plus overnight to chill | Serves 2

- 2 teaspoons chia seeds
- ½ cup almond milk, divided
- ½ teaspoon ground cinnamon, divided
- ½ teaspoon ground nutmeg, divided
- 2 tablespoons maple syrup, divided
- ½ cup rolled oats, gluten-free if needed, divided
- ½ cup pumpkin puree, divided
- ¼ cup plain 2% Greek yogurt, divided
- ¼ cup chopped walnuts, divided

1. Soften the chia seeds by putting 1 teaspoon in each jar, along with 2 tablespoons of milk in each jar.
2. Next, add ¼ teaspoon of cinnamon, ¼ teaspoon of nutmeg, and 1 tablespoon of maple syrup to each jar. Stir well. Let sit 15 minutes and stir again, so the chia doesn't clump.
3. Divide the oats and remaining milk evenly between the two jars. The oats should be saturated but not completely submerged.
4. Layer ¼ cup of the pumpkin puree, 2 tablespoons of Greek yogurt, and 2 tablespoons of walnuts on top of the oats in each jar.
5. Place the lids on the jars and chill overnight.

PER SERVING

Calories: 277 | Total fat: 13g | Sodium: 47mg | Carbohydrates: 35g | Fiber: 7g | Protein: 8g

Vegetable Cheddar Egg Muffins

Prep time: 10 minutes | Cook time: 15 minutes | Serves 4

- Cooking spray
- 8 eggs
- ½ cup grated cheddar cheese, or plant-based cheese
- 1 medium red bell pepper, chopped
- ½ teaspoon kosher salt, optional
- ½ teaspoon freshly ground black pepper, optional

1. Preheat the oven to 350°F. Lightly coat a 12-tin muffin pan with cooking spray or line it with muffin cups. (To avoid any metallic taste, use parchment paper muffin cups.)
2. In a large mixing bowl, beat the eggs. Then add the cheese, bell pepper, and salt and pepper (if using), and mix well. Divide the mixture evenly into the prepared muffin tins.
3. Bake the muffins until the tops are lightly golden, about 15 minutes. You may need to add 2 to 3 extra minutes of cooking time, depending on your oven.

PER SERVING

Calories: 210 | Total fat: 14g | Sodium: 234mg |
Carbohydrates: 3g | Fiber: 1g | Protein: 16g

Amazing Acai Breakfast Smoothie

Prep time: 5 minutes | Cook time: 5 minutes | Serves 2

- 2 (3.5-ounce) packets frozen acai puree
- 1 cup almond milk
- 1 frozen banana
- 2 tablespoons almond butter
- 2 tablespoons chia seeds
- 1 cup mixed frozen or fresh berries, such as blueberries, raspberries, strawberries, or blackberries, optional
- Ice, for thickness, optional

1. In a blender bowl, combine the frozen acai, almond milk, and banana, and blend on high until smooth.
2. Add the almond butter, chia seeds, and berries (if using), and blend for another 30 seconds. The mixture will thicken. Let it sit for a few minutes, and blend again.
3. Add ice and blend if you want a thicker smoothie, or add more almond milk for a thinner smoothie.
4. Pour the mixture into glasses, and enjoy.

PER SERVING

Calories: 304 | Total fat: 19g | Sodium: 77mg | Carbohydrates: 28g | Fiber: 10g | Protein: 8g

Blueberry Walnut Oatmeal

Prep time: 5 minutes | Cook time: 10 to 20 minutes | Serves 2

- 1 cup old-fashioned rolled oats, gluten-free if needed
- 2½ cups almond milk, divided
- 2 tablespoons ground flaxseed
- ¼ teaspoon ground cinnamon
- 1 cup fresh blueberries
- 4 tablespoons chopped walnuts
- 1 teaspoon maple syrup, optional

1. In a small pan, cook the oatmeal according to package instructions, using 2 cups of the almond milk. It should take 10 to 20 minutes, depending on the thickness you desire.
2. Place the oatmeal in a serving bowl. Pour the remaining ½ cup of almond milk over the oatmeal, and sprinkle in the flaxseed and cinnamon.
3. Top with blueberries and walnuts. Add maple syrup, if desired.

PER SERVING

Calories: 434 | Total fat: 18g | Sodium: 99mg | Carbohydrates: 59g | Fiber: 11g | Protein: 13g

Open-Faced Baked Eggs

Prep time: 15 minutes | Cook time: 40 minutes | Serves 4

- Cooking spray
- 4 slices whole-grain bread
- 1 tablespoon extra-virgin olive oil
- ½ medium yellow onion, chopped
- 1 cup sliced cremini mushrooms
- ½ cup chopped red bell pepper
- 4 cups baby spinach leaves
- 4 large eggs
- ½ teaspoon turmeric
- Kosher salt
- Freshly ground black pepper

1. Preheat the oven to 350°F, and coat a 9-by-13-inch baking pan with cooking spray.
2. While the oven preheats, toast the bread in a toaster oven until it is lightly browned. Then place the toasted bread in a single layer on the prepared pan.
3. In a large skillet, heat 1 tablespoon of olive oil over medium heat.
4. Add the chopped onion and sauté for 3 to 4 minutes until translucent.
5. Add the mushrooms and bell pepper and cook for 2 to 3 minutes, or until the mushrooms begin to brown.
6. Stir in the spinach and let it wilt for 2 to 3 minutes. Spread the vegetable mixture evenly over the toast in the baking pan.
7. Crack an egg over each piece of toast. Sprinkle the turmeric over the eggs. Bake for about 30 minutes, or until the egg whites are set and fully cooked.
8. Season to taste with salt and pepper.

PER SERVING

Calories: 193 | Total fat: 9g | Sodium: 235mg | Carbohydrates: 16g | Fiber: 4g | Protein: 12g

Baked Pears with Greek Yogurt

Prep time: 5 minutes | Cook time: 25 minutes | Cool time: 5 minutes | Serves 2

- 2 Bosc pears
- ½ teaspoon ground cinnamon
- ¼ cup crushed walnuts
- 2 tablespoons date or maple syrup
- 1 cup plain 2% Greek yogurt, or dairy-free option

1. Preheat the oven to 350°F, and line a baking sheet with parchment paper.
2. Cut the pears in half, discard the cores, then use a tablespoon to scoop a circle out of the center of each pear half.
3. Place the pears, circle-side up, on the baking sheet. Sprinkle the cinnamon over each pear half.
4. Divide the walnuts among the four halves. Drizzle the syrup evenly over each half.
5. Cook the pears for 25 minutes. Take them out of the oven and let them cool for 5 minutes. Top each pear half with ¼ cup of the Greek yogurt, and serve.

PER SERVING

Calories: 311 | Total fat: 12g | Sodium: 90mg | Carbohydrates: 47g | Fiber: 6g | Protein: 9g

Stovetop Steel-Cut Oats with Banana, Cherries, and Almonds

Prep time: 5 minutes | Cook time: 20 minutes | Cool time: 15 minutes | Serves 5

- 2 cups steel-cut oats
- 4½ cups almond or soy milk
- 1 large ripe banana, fresh or frozen
- 2 cups cherries, fresh or frozen, halved and pitted
- ½ cup slivered almonds, chopped

1. In a saucepan, combine the oats and milk, and bring to a boil over medium-high heat.
2. Reduce the heat to medium-low, and simmer for 15 minutes, or until the oats are soft.
3. Remove from the heat and add the banana. Cover the pot so that the banana softens in the trapped heat.
4. Mash or stir the softened banana into the oats until incorporated. Add the cherries and almonds, mixing to combine.
5. Cool the oats completely, then portion it into 5 screw-top glass jars, and garnish with more cherries or almonds, if desired.

PER SERVING

Calories: 380 | Total fat: 11g | Sodium: 150mg | Protein: 14g | Carbohydrates: 55g | Fiber: 9g

Tofu Breakfast Scramble

Prep time: 10 minutes | Cook time: 10 minutes | Serves 4

- 1 (14-ounce package) extra-firm tofu
- 2 teaspoons ground cumin
- 2 teaspoons turmeric
- 1 teaspoon freshly ground black pepper
- Kosher salt, optional
- 1 tablespoon extra-virgin olive oil
- 1 small yellow onion, chopped
- 4 to 5 garlic cloves, chopped
- 2 cups diced zucchini
- 2 cups sliced mushrooms
- 4 slices multigrain toast
- Fresh fruit, optional

1. Remove the tofu from its packaging, and press it by wrapping it in paper towels and placing something heavy, such as a pot or book, on top for about 5 minutes. This allows some of the excess liquid to drain out.
2. Place the tofu in a bowl, and crumble it with your hands. Stir in the cumin, turmeric, black pepper, and pinch of salt (if using). Set aside.
3. In a skillet, heat the olive oil over medium-high heat. Add the onion and garlic, and sauté for 5 minutes. Add the zucchini and mushrooms, and sauté for 3 minutes. Add the crumbled tofu, and sauté for 2 more minutes.
4. Serve immediately with a side of multigrain toast and/or fresh fruit (if using).

PER SERVING

Calories: 227 | Total fat: 11g | Sodium: 116mg | Carbohydrates: 21g | Fiber: 4g | Protein: 16g

Green Smoothie Bowl

Prep time: 15 minutes | Cook time: 5 minutes | Serves 2

- 3 cups packed baby spinach leaves
- 1 Granny Smith apple, cored
- 1 small ripe banana
- ½ ripe avocado
- 1 tablespoon maple syrup
- ½ cup mixed berries
- ¼ cup roasted slivered almonds, optional
- 1 teaspoon sesame seeds

1. In the bowl of a blender, combine the spinach, apple, banana, avocado, and maple syrup, and blend until smooth. The mixture should be thick.
2. Divide the mixture between two bowls. Top with the berries, almonds (if using), and sesame seeds, and serve.

PER SERVING

Calories: 280 | Total fat: 14g | Sodium: 40mg | Carbohydrates: 38g | Protein: 6g

Summer Vegetable Frittata

Prep time: 10 minutes | Cook time: 50 minutes | Rest time: 10 minutes | Serves 4

- 2 tablespoons extra-virgin olive oil
- 1 small red onion, thinly sliced
- 1 small zucchini, thinly sliced
- 1 (5-ounce) can artichoke hearts, drained and quartered
- 1 cup frozen corn, thawed
- ½ cup crumbled feta
- 1 teaspoon dried oregano
- ½ teaspoon kosher salt
- 10 large eggs, beaten

1. Preheat the oven to 375°F.
2. Coat the bottom of an 8-by-8-inch casserole dish with the oil. Arrange the onion and zucchini in an even layer in the dish.
3. Transfer the dish to the oven. Roast until the vegetables begin to caramelize, 5 to 7 minutes.
4. Add the artichoke hearts, corn, cheese, oregano, and salt. Gently pour the beaten eggs on top.
5. Return the dish to the oven. Bake until the eggs are firm but still jiggle a little when the dish is shaken, 25 to 35 minutes.
6. Remove from the oven, let rest for 10 minutes, and serve.

PER SERVING

Calories: 341 | Total fat: 24g | Sodium: 643mg | Carbohydrates: 15g | Fiber: 4g | Protein: 21g

Chapter 5
Lunches and Dinners

Raw Lasagna

Prep time: 20 minutes| Cook time: 35 minutes | Serves 12

- Walnut "Meatballs"
- Cashew Cheese
- 2 large zucchinis
- 1 tablespoon dried oregano, divided (for sprinkling)
- 1 cup fresh spinach
- 1 cup fresh basil
- 2 tablespoons extra-virgin olive oil

1. Prepare the Walnut "Meatballs" and the Cashew Cheese.
2. Peel and slice the zucchini into thin strips with a vegetable peeler. Place the first layer of zucchini in a deep lasagna dish (or 8 x 11 ½ x 2-inch baking dish) that holds 2 quarts.
3. Layer the zucchini so that the strips are just overlapping each other. You could also build the lasagna directly on plates if you will be eating it immediately. Sprinkle ½ tablespoon of oregano over the zucchini strips.
4. Layer ½ of the Walnut "Meatballs" over the zucchini.
5. Spread ½ cup Cashew Cheese over the Walnut "Meatballs."
6. Place ½ cup each of spinach and basil leaves over the Cashew Cheese.
7. Add another layer of zucchini strips. (Keep in mind that you will need 1 more layer for the top of the lasagna.)
8. Repeat the layering of the Walnut "Meatballs," Cashew Cheese, spinach, and basil.
9. Add the last layer of zucchini strips and sprinkle the remaining ½ tablespoon of oregano on top. Finish with a drizzle of extra-virgin olive oil.
10. The lasagna is now ready to eat, but if you allow it to set in the refrigerator overnight it will be easier to slice.

PER SERVING

Calories: 296.4 | Protein: 8g | Carbs: 15.9g | Dietary Fiber: 3.3g | Fat: 24g | Vitamin C: 15.3mg | Vitamin D: 0 IU | Vitamin E: 1mg | Calcium: 48.3mg | Iron: 2.6mg | Magnesium: 103.4mg | Potassium: 395.5mg

Zucchini Pasta with Broccoli Sprouts Pesto

Prep time: 10 minutes | Cook time: 25 minutes | Serves 4

- 4 zucchinis
- 1 cup fresh basil
- ½ cup broccoli sprouts
- Juice of 1 lemon
- 4 garlic cloves
- ½ teaspoon sea salt
- ½ cup spinach
- 2 cups raw walnuts
- ½ cup extra-virgin olive oil (or more for smoother mixture)

1. Make thin strips of zucchini using a vegetable peeler or pasta machine. Set aside.
2. Place the remaining ingredients in a blender and blend until the pesto mixture reaches desired consistency. Set aside.
3. Distribute the zucchini evenly among 4 plates.
4. Pour the pesto sauce over the zucchini pasta and serve.

PER SERVING

Calories: 683.1 | Protein: 12.5g | Carbs: 16.3g | Dietary Fiber: 6g | Fat: 67g | Vitamin C: 59.7mg | Vitamin D: 0 IU | Vitamin E: 4.3mg | Calcium: 145.6mg | Iron: 3.1mg | Magnesium: 142.2mg | Potassium: 899.4mg

Walnut "Meatballs"

Prep time: 10 minutes | Cook time: 10 minutes | Serves 4

- 1 ½ cups walnuts
- 1 cup sundried tomatoes
- 2 tablespoons extra-virgin olive oil
- 1 tablespoon fresh sage
- 1 teaspoon fennel seeds
- 1 teaspoon fresh thyme
- 1 teaspoon fresh rosemary
- 1 teaspoon fresh marjoram
- Pinch of black pepper
- Pinch of cayenne pepper
- Pinch of sea salt

1. Add all the ingredients to a blender and mix for 5 minutes or until well combined.

PER SERVING

Calories: 423 | Protein: 8.8g | Carbs: 20.5g | Dietary Fiber: 5.2g | Fat: 35.7g | Vitamin C: 8.2mg | Vitamin D: 0 IU | Vitamin E: 1.1mg | Calcium: 54.5mg | Iron: 2.1mg | Magnesium: 72.7mg | Potassium: 208.4mg

Cauliflower Crust Mini Pizzas

Cook time: 20 minutes | Cook time: 35 minutes | Serves 8

- 2 cups fresh cauliflower, steamed and grated
- 2 large pasture-raised eggs 2 cups grass-fed cheddar cheese
- 1 teaspoon toasted and ground fennel
- ¼ teaspoon sea salt
- 1 teaspoon ground oregano
- 2 teaspoon dried parsley
- 2 teaspoons dried basil
- 1 teaspoon dried rosemary
- 2 garlic cloves, minced
- Toppings of your choice:
- Raw Tomato Sauce
- Cheese (organic dairy or vegan)
- Pesto
- Tomatoes
- Olives

1. For the mini pizza crusts, steam the cauliflower, then grate, rice, or chop it finely. (You can do this in a food processor a few pieces at a time.)
2. Beat the eggs in a bowl, then add the cauliflower and shredded cheese and mix together.
3. Press 8 large spoonfuls of the cauliflower mixture onto a cookie sheet covered with parchment paper.
4. Sprinkle with the spices and bake at 450°F for 8 to 10 minutes. Keep the oven on.
5. To complete the pizzas, add desired pizza sauce (or a slice of fresh tomato) or pesto, and then add toppings such as cheese, grass-fed meat, olives, chopped mushrooms, etc. Just put back in oven until the cheese is melted for completed mini pizzas!

PER SERVING

Calories: 142.1 | Protein: 8.7g | Carbs: 3g | Dietary Fiber: 0.8g | Fat: 10.7g | Vitamin C: 13.4mg | Vitamin D: 17 IU | Vitamin E: 0.4mg | Calcium: 229.7mg | Iron: 0.8mg | Magnesium: 17.2mg | Potassium: 139.4mg

Crazy Sexy Bean Chili

Cook time: 15 minutes| Cook time: 45 minutes | Serves 8

- 1 ½ tablespoons cumin seeds
- 2 tablespoons olive oil
- 1 white onion, diced
- 3 garlic cloves, minced
- 1 jalapeño, finely diced (for less heat, remove the seeds and/or use ½ the pepper)
- 2 tablespoons chili powder
- 1 ½ cups ground seitan (alternatives: crumbled tempeh [wheat-free] or finely diced mushrooms [soy-free])
- 1 zucchini, diced
- ½ cup diced potato (any kind)
- Two 15-ounce cans black beans, rinsed
- One 15-ounce can kidney beans, rinsed
- One 14-ounce can crushed tomatoes (San Marzano recommended)
- 2 cups filtered water
- 2 tablespoons maple syrup
- 1 teaspoon sea salt
- ½ bunch of fresh cilantro
- 1 cup kale, chopped
- Diced avocado (optional)
- Fresh cilantro (optional)

1. Toast the cumin seeds in a dry soup pot on medium heat for 2 minutes, until you smell the robust aroma. (This process releases the full flavor of the spice.)
2. Add the olive oil, onion, garlic, and jalapeño. Stir constantly, until the onion is golden and translucent.
3. Add in the chili powder, seitan, zucchini, and potato and stir well. Sauté for 3 to 4 minutes, stirring to avoid sticking.
4. Add in the black beans, kidney beans, tomatoes, water, maple syrup, sea salt, and cilantro. Cover with a lid, reduce the heat to low, and allow the chili to cook for 20 to 25 minutes, or until the potatoes are tender.
5. Remove from the heat and stir in the kale.
6. Serve hot. Garnish with diced avocado and a handful of fresh cilantro, if desired.

PER SERVING

Calories: 288.8 | Protein: 17.5g | Carbs: 40.2g | Dietary Fiber: 11.8g | Fat: 8g | Vitamin C: 16.3mg | Vitamin D: 0 IU | Vitamin E: 2mg | Calcium: 109.3mg | Iron: 3.4mg | Magnesium: 62.8mg | Potassium: 994.4mg

Cauliflower Popcorn

Cook time: 15 minutes| Cook time: 25 minutes | Serves 4

- 2 ½ tablespoons extra-virgin olive oil
- ½ cup nutritional yeast
- ¾ teaspoon sea salt
- 1 head of cauliflower, chopped into bite-size pieces

1. Preheat the oven to 325°F.
2. Mix the olive oil, nutritional yeast, and sea salt thoroughly in a large bowl.
3. Add the cauliflower pieces to the bowl and toss until well coated.
4. Place the cauliflower on a baking sheet and bake for 20 minutes until golden brown and crispy.

PER SERVING

Calories: 144.4 | Protein: 6.6g | Carbs: 10g | Dietary Fiber: 4.4g | Fat: 9.4g | Vitamin C: 70.8mg | Vitamin D: 0 IU | Vitamin E: 1.2mg | Calcium: 35.3mg | Iron: 1mg | Magnesium: 33.1mg | Potassium: 571.5mg

Zucchini Spaghetti With Raw Tomato Sauce And Walnut "Meatballs"

Prep time: 5 minutes| Cook time: 35 minutes | Serves 4

- 2 large zucchinis
- 1 cup Raw Tomato Sauce
- 1 cup Walnut "Meatballs"
- Nutritional yeast, to taste upon serving (optional)

1. Use a spiralizer or vegetable peeler to make spaghetti strips with the zucchini. Place in bowls.
2. Make the Raw Tomato Sauce and pour over the zucchini spaghetti.
3. Make the Walnut "Meatballs" and add to the bowls. Sprinkle some nutritional yeast on top, if desired, and serve.

PER SERVING

Calories: 362.4 | Protein: 9.3g | Carbs: 34g | Dietary Fiber: 7.4g | Fat: 22.1g | Vitamin C: 53.8mg | Vitamin D: 0 IU | Vitamin E: 1.7mg | Calcium: 72.2mg | Iron: 2.9mg | Magnesium: 78mg | Potassium: 764.8mg

Anita Moorjani's Coconut Curry

Cook time: 10 minutes | Cook time: 25 minutes | Serves 4

- ½ red onion, coarsely chopped
- 4 garlic cloves, minced
- 1 tablespoon coconut oil or ghee
- 6 whole cloves
- 1 pound meat protein (chicken, beef, lamb), fish, or shrimp (optional)
- 4 cups vegetables of your choice, diced (squash, eggplant, zucchini, carrots, broccoli, string beans, baby corn, cauliflower, peas, or whatever else your favorites are!)
- 1 teaspoon turmeric powder
- 1 heaping teaspoon curry powder
- 1 cup coconut cream
- 1 stock cube dissolved in ¼ cup of warm filtered water (your choice of either chicken or vegetable stock, or freshly made stock)
- 1 ton love

1. Stir-fry the onions and garlic in the coconut oil or ghee until tender.
2. Add the cloves (and if you are adding meat, this is the point to do so).
3. Add the vegetables and stir-fry everything for another 2 to 3 minutes.
4. Add the turmeric powder and curry powder. Continue to stir-fry for another 2 to 3 minutes to allow the flavors to absorb. If you have added meat, continue to stir-fry until the meat is fully cooked.
5. Add the coconut cream, bring to boil, and allow to simmer for about 5 minutes.
6. Add ¼ cup stock and allow to simmer for another 15 minutes or longer. Anita says the longer you leave the curry to simmer, the better it tastes.
7. Serve on a bed of white or brown rice or quinoa, and add sea salt to taste.

PER SERVING

Calories: 345.1 | Protein: 2.7g | Carbs: 49.8g | Dietary Fiber: 3.1g | Fat: 16.1g | Vitamin C: 26.3mg | Vitamin D: 0 IU | Vitamin E: 0.6mg | Calcium: 42.8mg | Iron: 1mg | Magnesium: 34.9mg | Potassium: 459.6mg

Cauliflower Rice

Cook time: 10 minutes | Cook time: 15 minutes | Serves 4

- 1 head of cauliflower
- 1 tablespoon coconut oil
- Sea salt and pepper, to taste

1. Use a food processor to dice the cauliflower into tiny rice-size pieces.
2. Heat the oil in a pan, add the cauliflower, and sauté for 9 minutes. Season with sea salt and pepper.

PER SERVING

Calories: 66.7 | Protein: 2.8g | Carbs: 7.3g | Dietary Fiber: 2.9g | Fat: 3.6g | Vitamin C: 70.8mg | Vitamin D: 0 IU | Vitamin E: 0.1mg | Calcium: 32.3mg | Iron: 0.6mg | Magnesium: 22.5mg | Potassium: 439.5mg

Chickpea Burgers

Cook time: 5 minutes | Cook time: 15 minutes | Serves 4

- One 14-ounce can chickpeas, drained
- 2 teaspoons crushed garlic
- 1 teaspoon sea salt
- 1 teaspoon onion powder
- ¼ teaspoon cumin seeds
- ½ teaspoon cumin powder
- ¼ teaspoon turmeric
- ¼ teaspoon fennel
- ¼ teaspoon sage
- ¼ teaspoon rosemary
- ⅛ teaspoon oregano
- ¼ cup brown rice flour
- 1 tablespoon flax meal
- 2 tablespoons extra-virgin olive oil, for cooking
- ¼ teaspoon turmeric
- ¼ teaspoon black pepper

1. Place the chickpeas in a bowl and mash them so there are no chunks.
2. Add the rest of the ingredients to the chickpeas and mix well. You can use your hands for this. Make sure the mixture is well combined.
3. Form 4 patties.
4. Heat the pan to medium with olive oil and sauté the remaining ¼ teaspoon turmeric and black pepper for 1 minute or until sizzling until it becomes a thicker paste.
5. Spread the paste out over the pan and then add the patties. Cook for 4 minutes on each side or until golden brown.

PER SERVING

Calories: 210.6 | Protein: 6.1g | Carbs: 23.6g | Dietary Fiber: 5.6 | Fat: 10.2g | Vitamin C: 1.1mg | Vitamin D: 0 IU | Vitamin E: 0.9mg | Calcium: 49mg | Iron: 2mg | Magnesium: 2.3mg | Potassium: 24.5mg

Black Bean Bowl with Sweet Potatoes and Roasted Chickpeas

Cook time: 10 minutes | Cook time: 35 minutes | Serves 4

- Two 15-ounce cans black beans, drained and rinsed
- Sea salt and black pepper to taste
- ½ teaspoon cumin, divided
- ¼ teaspoon paprika
- Roasted Sweet Potato and Chickpeas:
- 2 sweet potatoes, cubed
- ½ teaspoon cumin
- ¼ teaspoon chili powder, divided
- ¼ teaspoon turmeric
- Sea salt and black pepper to taste
- One 15-ounce can chickpeas, drained and rinsed
- 2 cups of cooked quinoa or 4 servings of Cauliflower Rice
- ½ cup fresh cilantro
- 1 avocado, sliced
- Handful of broccoli sprouts
- 1 lime

1. Preheat the oven to 400°F.
2. Add the black beans to a pot with water so that the beans are just covered with a quarter-inch of water above, and bring to a rolling boil, then simmer for 4 minutes.
3. Season with sea salt, black pepper, cumin, and paprika, adding more to taste if you like. Set aside.
4. Make the seasoning for the sweet potatoes and chickpeas by adding all spices to a bowl and mix until well combined.
5. Place the sweet potato cubes on a baking sheet. Sprinkle with half the seasoning. Add 1 tablespoon water to glaze the potatoes and place in the oven. Bake for 10 minutes.
6. Toss the chickpeas to the other half of the seasoning, and then add the chickpeas to the potatoes on the baking sheet.
7. Bake an additional 15 to 20 minutes until the sweet potatoes are soft and the chickpeas crunchy.
8. Serve over quinoa, Cauliflower Rice or as nachos and eat with plantain or tortilla chips. Top with your favorite chipotle sauce, Taco Sauce or Fresh Fermented Salsa, fresh cilantro, sliced avocado, broccoli sprouts, and a squeeze of lime. Enjoy!

PER SERVING

Calories: 442.1 | Protein: 20.9g | Carbs: 71g | Dietary Fiber: 25.3g | Fat: 9.1g | Vitamin C: 18.3mg | Vitamin D: 0 IU | Vitamin E: 1.54mg | Calcium: 144.3mg | Iron: 4.9mg | Magnesium: 49.7mg | Potassium: 1,488mg

Bean Burgers

Cook time: 10 minutes| Cook time: 25 minutes | Serves 4

- One 15-ounce can organic beans (butter beans or black beans work best; or you can soak dry beans overnight, then boil them for an hour or until soft instead of using canned)
- ½ cup almond meal (blended almond)
- 1 small yellow onion, chopped
- 1 tablespoon nutritional yeast
- 2 tablespoons broccoli sprouts, diced
- 1 teaspoon black seeds
- ½ teaspoon cumin
- ¼ teaspoon garlic powder
- ¼ teaspoon fennel
- ¼ teaspoon thyme
- ¼ teaspoon sage
- ¼ teaspoon sea salt
- ¼ teaspoon black pepper
- ⅛ teaspoon turmeric
- Pinch of cayenne pepper
- 1 Flax Egg Alternative
- 2 tablespoons extra-virgin coconut oil

1. Drain the beans. Mash the beans in a bowl and mix in the remaining ingredients, except for the oil.
2. Taste the mixture and add more spices or sea salt to your liking.
3. Divide the mixture into 4 equal parts and shape into 4 patties.
4. Heat the oil in a large pan over medium heat. Fry the patties until golden, about 4 to 5 minutes on each side.
5. Serve on Gluten Free Tortillas, or Teff Crepes kale, collard greens, or lettuce. The burgers taste great with herbs like fresh parsley, cilantro, and basil.

PER SERVING

Calories: 278.4 | Protein: 11.7g | Carbs: 25.9g | Dietary Fiber: 10.8g | Fat: 15.2g | Vitamin C: 9.1mg | Vitamin D: 0 IU | Vitamin E: 4.4mg | Calcium: 94.9mg | Iron: 2.9mg | Magnesium: 45.7mg | Potassium: 529.1mg

Cajun Spice Pasta With Oat Cream

Cook time: 15 minutes| Cook time: 45 minutes | Serves 4

- 4 small chicken breasts
- 2 tablespoons extra-virgin olive oil plus more for the chicken breasts
- 5 teaspoons Cajun spice (a mix of garlic, paprika, sea salt, black pepper, cayenne pepper, onion, thyme, and Italian seasoning [parsley, oregano, rosemary, thyme]), divided
- 2 cups gluten-free pasta (brown rice, lentil, chickpea, or bean)
- 1 red pepper, sliced
- 1 brown onion, sliced
- 2 garlic cloves, sliced
- 2 cups vegetable stock
- 1 cup oat cream or milk (can also use coconut cream)
- ¼ teaspoon chili pepper
- 2 cups mixed greens
- 2 cups fresh spinach

1. Preheat the oven to 350°F. Place the chicken breasts on a baking sheet. Drizzle each with oil and then sprinkle a teaspoon of Cajun spice on each along with a dash of sea salt and pepper.
2. Bake for 25 to 30 minutes or until chicken is cooked through.
3. Meanwhile, make the brown rice pasta according to package instructions.
4. Sauté the pepper, onion, and garlic in olive oil. Once cooked, stir in the vegetable stock and oat milk.
5. Add the chili and the remaining 1 teaspoon Cajun spice. Add the pasta and stir to combine well for a couple of minutes. Divide the mixture among 4 plates and place 1 chicken breast atop each.
6. Serve with a crisp salad drizzled with olive oil, sea salt, and pepper.

PER SERVING

Calories: 565.6 | Protein: 51.9g | Carbs: 48.4g | Dietary Fiber: 1.8g | Fat: 18.3g | Vitamin C: 51.4mg | Vitamin D: 26.7 IU | Vitamin E: . 3.1mg | Calcium: 175.7mg | Iron: 5mg | Magnesium: 65.4mg | Potassium: 749.4mg

Broccoli In Creamy Pea Pesto

Cook time: 5 minutes| Cook time: 15 minutes | Serves 4

- 1 ½ cups frozen peas
- 1 ½ cups basil leaves
- 2 small garlic cloves (or 1 large)
- 2 tablespoons almond flour
- 3 tablespoons olive oil
- ½ teaspoon sea salt
- ¼ teaspoon cayenne powder (optional)
- 4 cups broccoli florets (just the top ¾ inch)
- Pinch of sea salt
- Broccoli sprouts
- Basil leaves
- Red pepper flakes

1. Combine all the pesto ingredients in a blender, and blend on high speed until the mixture is smooth. Set aside.
2. Bring a large pot of water with a pinch of sea salt to a boil. Fill a large bowl with water and 2 cups of ice and place on the side.
3. Add the broccoli florets to the pot of boiling water, cook for 90 seconds to 2 minutes, until bright green. Use a slotted spoon to transfer the broccoli to the ice bath to cool down and stop cooking.
4. After 2 minutes, drain the broccoli, then add to a dry bowl along with the pesto and mix well.
5. You can enjoy this dish at room temperature or gently warm the pesto broccoli in a dry pan over low heat, if desired.
6. Top with or stir in broccoli sprouts, basil leaves, and red pepper flakes, if desired, before serving.

PER SERVING

Calories: 183.4 | Protein: 6.5g | Carbs: 12.4g | Dietary Fiber: 4.7g | Fat: 12.9g | Vitamin C: 87.1mg | Vitamin D: 0 IU | Vitamin E: 2.4mg | Calcium: 103mg | Iron: 2.3mg | Magnesium: 55.4mg | Potassium: 404.3mg

Chapter 6
Soothing Soups

Spiced Squash Soup

Prep time: 10 minutes | Cook time: 35 minutes | Serves 6 to 8

- 2 tablespoons extra-virgin olive oil
- 1 medium onion, diced
- ½ teaspoon sea salt, divided
- ½ teaspoon ground ginger
- ¼ teaspoon ground cinnamon
- ¼ teaspoon ground cardamom
- ¼ teaspoon chili powder
- ¼ teaspoon ground nutmeg
- 3 large carrots, cut into small chunks
- 1 large parsnip, peeled and cut into small chunks
- 1 large winter squash (about 3 pounds), peeled, seeded, and cut into small chunks
- ¼ teaspoon dried thyme
- 3 garlic cloves, minced or pressed
- 1 (2-inch) piece of fresh ginger, peeled and minced
- 6 to 8 cups vegetable broth (such as Mineral-Rich Vegetable Broth)

1. Heat the olive oil in a Dutch oven or large, deep pot over medium heat.
2. Add the onion, ¼ teaspoon of the salt, the ground ginger, cinnamon, cardamom, chili powder, and nutmeg and sauté until the onion is translucent, about 3 minutes.
3. Add the carrots, parsnip, and squash, stir to combine, and cook until the vegetables begin to brown and soften, about 10 minutes. Add the remaining ¼ teaspoon of salt along with the thyme, garlic, and fresh ginger and stir to combine.
4. Add 6 cups of the broth and stir to combine. Bring to a boil, then reduce the heat to medium-low and cover. Cook for approximately 20 minutes, until the vegetables are tender.
5. Puree the soup with an immersion blender (or in a blender, working in batches) until smooth and creamy, adding more broth as needed to achieve your preferred consistency.
6. Serve warm. Store leftovers in an airtight container in the refrigerator for up to 1 week or in the freezer for up to 3 months.

PER SERVING

Calories: 174 | Total fat: 5g | Sodium: 241mg | Carbohydrates: 34g | Fiber: 6g | Protein: 3g

Black Bean Soup

Prep time: 10 minutes | Cook time: 20 minutes | Serves 4

- 2 tablespoons extra-virgin olive oil
- 1 medium onion, finely chopped
- 1 celery stalk, diced
- 2 garlic cloves, minced or pressed
- 1½ teaspoons dry mustard
- ¼ teaspoon ground cloves
- 5 cups vegetable broth (such as Mineral-Rich Vegetable Broth)
- 3 (15-ounce) cans black beans, rinsed and drained
- 2 dried bay leaves
- ½ teaspoon sea salt, or more as needed
- 1 cup crème fraîche or plain full-fat Greek yogurt
- Freshly ground black pepper
- 1 avocado, pitted, peeled, and diced

1. In a Dutch oven or large, deep pot, heat the oil over medium heat, then add the onion, celery, and garlic. Cook for about 3 minutes, stirring occasionally, until the onion is translucent.
2. Stir in the mustard and cloves. Add 1 cup of the broth and simmer until the onion is softened, about 2 minutes. Then add the beans, another 3 cups of the broth, bay leaves, and salt. Cook until heated through and fragrant, about 15 minutes.
3. Remove the soup from the heat, discard the bay leaves, and puree with an immersion blender (or in a blender, working in batches) until smooth and creamy.
4. Add more broth, if needed, to achieve your desired consistency. Stir in the crème fraîche and season to taste with salt and pepper.
5. Serve warm, topped with the avocado. Store leftovers in an airtight container in the refrigerator for up to 1 week or in the freezer for up to 3 months.

PER SERVING

Calories: 430 | Total fat: 17g | Sodium: 290mg | Carbohydrates: 53g | Fiber: 20g | Protein: 20g

Roasted Butternut Squash, Apple, and Sage Soup

Prep time: 10 minutes | Cook time: 50 minutes | Serves 4

- 1 large butternut squash (3 to 4 pounds), halved lengthwise, seeds removed
- 2 large shallots, quartered
- 2 medium to large apples, peeled, cored, and quartered
- 1 (1-inch) piece of fresh ginger, peeled and cut into thirds
- 2 tablespoons extra-virgin olive oil
- 1 cup canned full-fat coconut milk
- 8 fresh sage leaves, or 1 tablespoon ground
- ½ teaspoon sea salt, or more as desired
- Toasted pepitas or almond slices, for garnish (optional)

1. Preheat the oven to 400°F. Line a baking sheet with parchment paper.
2. Place the squash cut side down on the baking sheet and add the shallots, apples, and ginger in a single layer.
3. Drizzle with the olive oil and use your hands to coat the ingredients. Cover the baking sheet with a large piece of foil, sealing around the edges.
4. Roast until the apples are tender, about 30 minutes. Remove the apples from the baking sheet, along with the shallots and ginger.
5. Reseal the baking sheet with the foil and roast the squash for another 20 minutes, or until soft enough to be easily pierced with a fork. Let it cool.
6. When cool enough to handle, scoop out the flesh from the squash and place in a food processor or high-speed blender.
7. Add the apples, shallots, and ginger, then add the coconut milk, sage, and salt. Blend until smooth. If the mixture is too thick, add warm water a tablespoon at a time until you reach the desired consistency. Adjust the salt to taste.
8. Pour the soup into bowls and sprinkle with pepitas or almond slices, if using. Serve immediately. Store leftovers in an airtight container in the refrigerator for up to 1 week or in the freezer for up to 3 months.

PER SERVING

Calories: 367 | Total fat: 19g | Sodium: 254mg | Carbohydrates: 53g | Fiber: 8g | Protein: 5g

Moroccan-Inspired Vegetable Soup with Chickpeas

Prep time: 10 minutes | Cook time: 25 minutes | Serves 6

- 2 tablespoons extra-virgin olive oil
- 1 large onion, chopped
- 2 celery stalks, chopped
- 1 medium sweet potato, peeled and cut into ½-inch cubes
- 1 large carrot, diced
- 2 large garlic cloves, minced or pressed
- 1½ teaspoons ground cumin
- 1 teaspoon ground turmeric
- ½ teaspoon ground coriander
- ½ teaspoon ground cinnamon
- ½ teaspoon sea salt
- ¼ teaspoon freshly ground black pepper
- Pinch saffron
- 6 cups vegetable broth (such as Mineral-Rich Vegetable Broth)
- 2 (15-ounce) cans chickpeas, rinsed and drained
- 1 lemon, cut into wedges

1. In a Dutch oven or large, deep pot, heat the oil over medium heat. Add the onion and celery and sauté until golden, about 6 minutes. Add the sweet potato and carrot and sauté until starting to soften, another 3 minutes.
2. Stir in the garlic, cumin, turmeric, coriander, cinnamon, salt, pepper, and saffron and cook for another minute.
3. Pour in ½ cup of the broth to deglaze the pot, stirring and scraping with a wooden spoon to get up the browned bits.
4. Add the chickpeas and the remaining 5½ cups of broth. Bring to a boil, reduce the heat to low, cover, and simmer until the vegetables are soft, about 15 minutes.
5. Puree the soup with an immersion blender (or in a blender, working in batches). I enjoy this soup partially pureed, with some pieces of vegetables and chickpeas still whole.
6. Serve warm with a squeeze of fresh lemon juice. Store leftovers in an airtight container in the refrigerator for up to 1 week or in the freezer for up to 3 months.

PER SERVING
Calories: 256 | Total fat: 8g | Sodium: 421mg | Carbohydrates: 38g | Fiber: 10g | Protein: 10g

Chicken Tortilla Soup

Prep time: 10 minutes | Cook time: 20 minutes | Serves 4 to 6

- 2 tablespoons extra-virgin olive oil
- 1 small onion, chopped
- 3 garlic cloves, minced or pressed
- 4 cups bone broth (such as Mineral-Rich Bone Broth, or Basic Chicken Bone Broth)
- 1 (14.5-ounce) can diced tomatoes
- 1 pound boneless, skinless chicken breasts
- ¾ tablespoon ground cumin
- ½ tablespoon chili powder
- ½ teaspoon sea salt
- 2 medium carrots, thinly sliced
- ½ cup chopped fresh cilantro, plus more for garnish
- Juice of 1 lime, plus more for serving
- Tortilla chips
- 2 avocados, pitted, peeled and diced
- Shredded cheddar or Monterey Jack cheese (optional)

1. In a Dutch oven or large, deep pot, heat the oil over medium-high heat. Add the onion and garlic and sauté until softened, about 3 minutes.
2. Add the broth, tomatoes with their juice, chicken, cumin, chili powder, and salt. Submerge the chicken in the liquid, increase the heat to high, and bring to a boil.
3. Add the carrots. Return to a boil, then reduce the heat to medium and cook for another 10 to 12 minutes, until the carrots are tender.
4. Using tongs, carefully remove the chicken from the pot and either shred or chop it. Put the chicken back in the pot and stir in the cilantro and lime juice.
5. Ladle the soup into bowls and serve topped with a handful of tortilla chips, avocado, more cilantro, cheese (if using), and a spritz more lime juice.
6. Store any leftovers, without the toppings, in an airtight container in the refrigerator for up to 1 week or in the freezer for up to 4 months.

PER SERVING

Calories: 428 | Total fat: 26g | Sodium: 387mg | Carbohydrates: 23g | Fiber: 12g | Protein: 31g

Aromatic Lentil Soup

Prep time: 10 minutes | Cook time: 45 minutes | Serves 8

- 1 tablespoon extra-virgin olive oil
- 2 medium onions, chopped (about 2 cups)
- 2 large carrots, chopped (about 2 cups)
- 4 garlic cloves, minced or pressed
- 1 teaspoon ground cumin
- 1 teaspoon ground coriander
- 1 teaspoon ground turmeric
- ½ teaspoon ground cinnamon
- ½ teaspoon sea salt
- ¼ teaspoon freshly ground black pepper
- 8 cups vegetable broth (such as Mineral-Rich Vegetable Broth)
- ½ head cauliflower, cored and chopped
- 2 cups green or brown lentils, rinsed
- 1 (28-ounce) can diced tomatoes
- 2 tablespoons tomato paste
- 4 cups chopped fresh spinach, or 1 (10-ounce) package frozen spinach, thawed
- Chopped fresh cilantro, for garnish
- Fresh lemon juice

1. In a Dutch oven or large, deep pot, heat the oil over medium heat, then add the onions and carrots.
2. Cook, stirring occasionally, until softened, about 10 minutes. Stir in the garlic and cook for about 30 seconds.
3. Add the cumin, coriander, turmeric, cinnamon, salt, and pepper. Cook, stirring, until fragrant, about 1 minute.
4. Add the broth, cauliflower, lentils, tomatoes with their juice, and tomato paste, then increase the heat to high and bring to a boil.
5. Reduce the heat to low, cover partially, and simmer until the lentils are tender but not mushy, 30 to 40 minutes. Stir in the spinach and cook until just wilted, 3 to 4 minutes.
6. Serve warm, sprinkled with cilantro and drizzled with lemon juice. Store leftovers in an airtight container in the refrigerator for up to 1 week or in the freezer for up to 3 months.

PER SERVING

Calories: 240 | Total fat: 3g | Sodium: 273mg | Carbohydrates: 43g | Fiber: 10g | Protein: 15g

Spring Green Soup

Prep time: 10 minutes | Cook time: 20 minutes | Serves 4 to 6

- 2 tablespoons extra-virgin olive oil
- 1 leek, white and light green parts only, thinly sliced
- ½ teaspoon sea salt, or more as needed
- 4 cups frozen peas, thawed, or 3½ pounds fresh peas, shelled
- 4 cups vegetable broth (such as Mineral-Rich Vegetable Broth)
- 2 cups tightly packed fresh baby spinach
- ¼ cup chopped fresh flat-leaf parsley
- ¼ cup chopped fresh mint
- ¼ cup chopped fresh chives
- 1 cup plain full-fat Greek yogurt
- 1 teaspoon lemon juice

1. In a Dutch oven or large, deep pot, heat the oil over medium heat. Add the leek and salt, cover, and cook until soft and tender, stirring occasionally, about 10 minutes.
2. Add the peas, pour in the broth, and bring to a simmer. Cover and cook until the peas are tender but still bright green, 5 to 8 minutes for frozen peas, 20 to 25 minutes for fresh peas.
3. Stir in the spinach, parsley, mint, and chives and cook for about 1 minute, until the greens are wilted.
4. Puree the soup with an immersion blender (or in a blender, working in batches). Stir in the yogurt and lemon juice and add more salt, if needed.
5. Serve warm, at room temperature, or chilled. Store leftovers in an airtight container in the refrigerator for up to 5 days or in the freezer for up to 3 months.

PER SERVING

Calories: 234 | Total fat: 10g | Sodium: 287mg | Carbohydrates: 28g | Fiber: 8g | Protein: 11g

Veggie Lover's Chicken Soup

Prep time: 10 minutes | Cook time: 20 minutes | Serves 4

- 2 tablespoons extra-virgin olive oil
- 1 pound boneless, skinless chicken breasts, cut into bite-size pieces
- 2 medium zucchini, diced
- 2 large shallots, finely chopped
- 1 teaspoon herbes de Provence
- ¼ teaspoon sea salt
- 4 ripe plum tomatoes, chopped
- 4 cups bone broth (such as Mineral-Rich Bone Broth, or Basic Chicken Bone Broth)
- ½ cup dry white wine or apple cider vinegar
- ¼ cup orzo, orecchiette, ditalini, or other tiny pasta
- 2 cups chopped fresh spinach
- Fresh lemon juice
- Grated Parmesan or Romano cheese (optional)

1. In a Dutch oven or large, deep pot, heat the oil over medium-high heat.
2. Add the chicken and cook until browned all over and cooked through, 3 to 4 minutes. Transfer to a plate.
3. Add the zucchini, shallots, herbes de Provence, and salt to the pot.
4. Cook, stirring often, until the veggies are slightly softened, about 3 minutes.
5. Add the tomatoes, broth, wine, and orzo. Increase the heat to high and bring to a boil.
6. Reduce to low and simmer until the pasta is tender, about 10 minutes.
7. Stir in the spinach and chicken. Simmer for another 5 minutes.
8. Serve with a squeeze of lemon juice and some grated Parmesan, if using. Store leftovers in an airtight container in the refrigerator for up to 4 days or in the freezer for up to 4 months.

PER SERVING

Calories: 260 | Total fat: 10g | Sodium: 193mg | Carbohydrates: 12g | Fiber: 3g | Protein: 28g

Pumpkin Curry Soup

Prep time: 5 minutes | Cook time: 25 minutes | Serves 4

- 1 tablespoon unsalted butter (preferably grass-fed)
- 1 large onion, chopped
- 2 garlic cloves, minced or pressed
- 2 teaspoons peeled and minced fresh ginger
- 1½ teaspoons curry powder
- 1 teaspoon ground cumin
- ½ teaspoon ground coriander
- ½ teaspoon ground cinnamon
- ½ teaspoon sea salt
- 4 cups vegetable broth (such as Mineral-Rich Vegetable Broth)
- 2 dried bay leaves
- 2 (15-ounce) cans pumpkin puree
- ¼ cup heavy cream
- Freshly ground black pepper
- Toasted pepitas, for garnish

1. In a Dutch oven or deep saucepan, heat the butter over medium heat. Add the onion and cook, stirring, until soft and translucent, about 5 minutes.
2. Add the garlic and ginger and cook, stirring, for another minute. Stir in the curry, cumin, coriander, cinnamon, and salt and sauté for 2 minutes more.
3. Add the broth, bay leaves, and pumpkin puree to the Dutch oven. Stir to combine, increase the heat to high, and bring to a boil. Reduce to low and simmer, covered, for 15 minutes.
4. Remove the bay leaves and puree the soup with an immersion blender (or in a blender, working in batches). Stir in the cream and add pepper to taste.
5. Serve warm, topped with toasted pumpkin seeds, if using. Store leftovers in an airtight container in the refrigerator for up to 1 week or in the freezer for up to 3 months.

PER SERVING

Calories: 200 | Total fat: 9g | Sodium: 376mg | Carbohydrates: 31g | Fiber: 3g | Protein: 4g

Mushroom Barley Soup

Prep time: 25 minutes | Cook time: 45 minutes | Serves 4

- ½ ounce dried porcini mushrooms
- ½ ounce dried shiitake mushrooms
- 4 cups boiling water
- 3 tablespoons extra-virgin olive oil
- 1 medium onion, diced
- 12 ounces fresh cremini or white button mushrooms, sliced
- 1 carrot, diced
- 1 celery stalk, sliced
- 2 garlic cloves, minced or pressed
- 1 teaspoon dried thyme, or 1 tablespoon minced fresh
- 4 cups vegetable broth (such as Mineral-Rich Vegetable Broth)
- ½ cup pearl barley
- 1 teaspoon sea salt
- ½ teaspoon freshly ground black pepper

1. Place the porcini and shiitake mushrooms in a medium bowl and pour the boiling water over. Cover with plastic wrap or a plate and let soak for 20 minutes.
2. Strain the mushrooms through a fine-mesh sieve over a bowl and reserve the liquid. Finely chop the mushrooms.
3. In a Dutch oven or large, deep pot, heat the olive oil over medium-high heat. Add the onion and cook for about 4 minutes, until translucent.
4. Stir in the cremini mushrooms, carrot, and celery and cook until tender, 5 to 6 minutes. Add the garlic and thyme, stir to combine, and cook until fragrant, about 30 seconds more.
5. Add ½ cup of the broth to deglaze the pot, stirring and scraping with a wooden spoon to get up the browned bits. Stir until the liquid is reduced by half, about 3 minutes.
6. Add the soaked mushrooms, reserved mushroom water, remaining 3½ cups of broth, barley, salt, and pepper.
7. Bring to a simmer, reduce the heat to low, and cook for 35 to 40 minutes, until the barley is tender.
8. Serve warm. Store leftovers in an airtight container in the refrigerator for up to 1 week or in the freezer for up to 3 months. I think this soup tastes even better after a few days.

PER SERVING

Calories: 238 | Total fat: 11g | Sodium: 488mg | Carbohydrates: 32g | Fiber: 7g | Protein: 6g

Lemony Chicken Soup

Prep time: 10 minutes | Cook time: 20 minutes | Serves 5

- 2 tablespoons extra-virgin olive oil
- 1 medium onion, quartered and thinly sliced
- 4 garlic cloves, minced or pressed
- 10 cups bone broth (such as Mineral-Rich Bone Broth, or Basic Chicken Bone Broth)
- 1 pound boneless, skinless chicken breasts
- Grated zest and juice of 1 large lemon
- ½ teaspoon red pepper flakes
- 1 cup Israeli couscous
- 1 teaspoon sea salt, or more as needed
- ½ teaspoon freshly ground black pepper, or more as needed
- ½ cup crumbled feta cheese (about 3 ounces)
- ⅓ cup chopped fresh chives

1. In a large Dutch oven or large, deep pot, heat the oil over medium-high heat. Add the onion and garlic and sauté for 3 to 4 minutes to soften.
2. Add the broth, chicken, lemon zest and juice, and red pepper flakes. Increase the heat to high, cover, and bring to a boil. Once boiling, reduce the heat to medium and simmer, uncovered, for 10 minutes.
3. Stir in the couscous, salt, and pepper. Simmer for another 5 minutes to cook the couscous, then turn off the heat.
4. Using tongs, carefully remove the chicken from the pot and either shred or chop it. Put the chicken back in the pot, stir in the feta and chives, then taste and add more salt or pepper, if desired.
5. Serve. Store leftovers in an airtight container in the refrigerator for up to 1 week or in the freezer for up to 4 months.

PER SERVING

Calories: 346 | Total fat: 12g | Sodium: 551mg | Carbohydrates: 31g | Fiber: 2g | Protein: 28g

Harira-Inspired Stew

Prep time: 10 minutes | Cook time: 2 hours | Serves 8

- 2 tablespoons extra-virgin olive oil
- 1 teaspoon ground turmeric
- 1 teaspoon ground ginger
- 1 teaspoon ground cinnamon
- 1 teaspoon sea salt
- ½ teaspoon freshly ground black pepper
- Large pinch saffron
- 3 celery stalks, finely chopped (about 1 cup)
- 2 medium onions, finely chopped
- 6 garlic cloves, minced or pressed
- 1 cup chopped fresh flat-leaf parsley
- 1 pound boneless, skinless chicken thighs, cut into bite-size cubes
- 1 (28-ounce) can diced tomatoes
- 1½ cups cooked chickpeas, or 1 (15-ounce) can chickpeas, rinsed and drained
- ¾ cup green or brown lentils, rinsed
- 4 cups bone broth (such as Mineral-Rich Bone Broth, or Basic Chicken Bone Broth)
- 4 cups water
- Lemon, cut into quarters

1. In a Dutch oven or large, deep pot, heat the olive oil over medium heat.
2. Add the turmeric, ginger, cinnamon, salt, pepper, saffron, celery, onions, garlic, and parsley. Cook, stirring occasionally, until the vegetables soften, about 10 minutes.
3. Add the chicken and stir to combine. Continue to cook for another 10 minutes.
4. Add the tomatoes with their juice, chickpeas, lentils, broth, and water.
5. Increase the heat to high and bring to a boil. Reduce the heat to low, cover, and simmer until the flavors are melded, about 90 minutes.
6. Serve the stew warm with a squeeze of fresh lemon juice.
7. Store leftovers in an airtight container in the refrigerator for up to 1 week or in the freezer for up to 4 months.

PER SERVING

Calories: 266 | Total fat: 8g | Sodium: 421mg | Carbohydrates: 30g | Fiber: 8g | Protein: 21g

Chapter 7
Vital Vegetables

Basil Broccoli

Prep time: 10 minutes | Cook time: 5 minutes | Serves 4

- 1 bunch of broccoli
- Sea salt
- 2 tablespoons extra-virgin olive oil
- 1 tablespoon finely chopped garlic
- Pinch of red pepper flakes
- ½ cup halved cherry tomatoes or diced red bell pepper
- 1 tablespoon freshly squeezed lemon juice
- 2 teaspoons lemon zest
- ¼ cup fresh basil, finely chopped

1. Bring a large pot of water to a boil. Cut the broccoli florets off the stalks, then peel the stems and cut them into bite-size pieces.
2. Add a pinch of salt and the broccoli florets and stems to the pot of water and blanch for 30 seconds. Drain the broccoli, then run it under cold water to stop the cooking process; this will retain its lush green color.
3. Heat the olive oil in a sauté pan over medium heat, then add the garlic and red pepper flakes and sauté for 30 seconds, just until aromatic.
4. Add the cherry tomatoes and a pinch of salt and sauté for an additional minute. Stir in the broccoli florets and ¼ teaspoon of salt and sauté for 2 minutes; the broccoli should still be firm.
5. Gently stir in the lemon juice, lemon zest, and basil and serve immediately.

PER SERVING

Calories: 125 | Total Fat: 7.7g | Sat Fat: 1.1g | Carbohydrates: 13g | Protein: 5g | Fiber: 5g | Sodium: 125mg

Baby Bok Choy with Yam and Ginger

Prep time: 15 minutes | Cook time: 5 minutes | Serves 6

- 4 heads baby bok choy
- 2 tablespoons light sesame oil
- 2 scallions, white part only, thinly sliced
- 2 tablespoons minced fresh ginger
- 1 cup peeled and finely diced Garnet sweet potato or yam
- Sea salt
- 1 tablespoon tamari
- 1 teaspoon maple syrup
- 1 tablespoon freshly squeezed lime juice, plus more to taste
- ¼ teaspoon toasted sesame oil (optional)

1. Trim the bases off the bok choy and discard. Trim the leaves from the stems and cut both crosswise into bite-size pieces, keeping the stems and leaves separate.
2. Heat the light sesame oil in a sauté pan over medium heat, then add the scallions and ginger and sauté for 30 seconds. Add the sweet potato and a pinch of salt and sauté for an additional minute.
3. Add the bok choy stems, tamari, and maple syrup and sauté for 2 minutes more. Add the bok choy leaves, lime juice, ¼ teaspoon of salt, and the toasted sesame oil.
4. Cook until the bok choy is just wilted, about 2 minutes, then taste: you may want to add a squeeze of lime if desired. Serve immediately.

PER SERVING

Calories: 150 | Total Fat: 6g | Sat Fat: 0.9g | Carbohydrates: 19g | Protein: 9g | Fiber: 6g | Sodium: 595mg

Green Beans with Brazil Nuts and Basil

Prep time: 15 minutes | Cook time: 10 minutes | Serves 6

- Sea salt
- 1 pound green beans, trimmed
- 2 tablespoons extra-virgin olive oil
- 2 tablespoons chopped shallot
- Freshly ground pepper
- Freshly squeezed lemon juice
- 2 tablespoons finely ground Brazil nuts or walnuts
- 2 tablespoons finely chopped fresh basil
- ½ teaspoon lemon zest

1. Bring a generous amount of water (about 8 cups) to a boil. Add ¼ teaspoon of salt and the green beans and cook until tender but still crisp, 3 to 6 minutes.
2. Drain the green beans, then run them under cold water to stop the cooking process.
3. Heat the olive oil in a large sauté pan over medium heat, then add the shallot and a pinch of salt and sauté until translucent, about 1 minute.
4. Stir in the beans, add ¼ teaspoon of salt, and cook, stirring occasionally, until heated through, about 2 minutes. Remove from the heat and add several grinds of pepper, a spritz of the lemon juice, and the nuts.
5. Toss with the basil and lemon zest before serving.

PER SERVING

Calories: 320 | Total Fat: 8.3g | Sat Fat: 1.1g | Carbohydrates: 47g | Protein: 18g | Fiber: 12g | Sodium: 110mg

Emerald Greens with Orange

Prep time: 10 minutes | Cook time: 10 minutes | Serves 4

- 2 tablespoons extra-virgin olive oil
- 1 teaspoon minced garlic
- Pinch of red pepper flakes
- 2 tablespoons dried cranberries
- ¼ cup freshly squeezed orange juice
- 6 cups stemmed and chopped Swiss chard, in bite-size pieces
- ¼ teaspoon sea salt
- ½ teaspoon orange zest
- ¼ teaspoon maple syrup

1. Heat the olive oil in a large sauté pan over medium heat, then add the garlic, red pepper flakes, cranberries, and orange juice and sauté for 30 seconds, just until aromatic.
2. Add the chard, salt, and orange zest and sauté until the color of the chard begins to darken and intensify.
3. Use a slotted spoon to transfer the greens to a bowl, then bring the liquid in the pan to a boil. When the liquid shrinks in from the sides of the pan and thickens a bit, stir the greens back in, then stir in the maple syrup.
4. Do a FASS check. You may want to add another pinch of salt. Serve immediately.

PER SERVING

Calories: 90 | Total Fat: 7.2g | Sat Fat: 1g | Carbohydrates: 7g | Protein: 1g | Fiber: 1g | Sodium: 260mg

Shredded Carrot and Beet Salad

Prep time: 10 minutes | Cook time: 10 minutes | Serves 4

- 2 tablespoons freshly squeezed orange juice
- 2 teaspoons freshly squeezed lemon juice
- 2 teaspoons extra-virgin olive oil
- ½ teaspoon minced fresh ginger
- ¼ teaspoon sea salt
- 1 cup peeled and shredded carrot
- 1 cup peeled and shredded red beet
- 2 tablespoons chopped fresh mint

1. Whisk the orange juice, lemon juice, olive oil, ginger, and salt together until thoroughly combined.
2. Put the carrots in a mixing bowl, drizzle with half of the dressing, and toss until evenly coated.
3. Place the carrots on one side of a shallow serving bowl. Put the beets in the mixing bowl, drizzle with the remaining dressing, and toss until evenly coated.
4. Place the beets in the serving bowl next to the carrots for a beautiful contrast of red and orange. Top with the chopped mint before serving.

PER SERVING

Calories: 50 | Total Fat: 2.5g | Sat Fat: 0.4g | Carbohydrates: 7g | Protein: 1g | Fiber: 2g | Sodium: 195 mg

Kale with Sweet Potatoes and Pecans

Prep time: 15 minutes | Cook time: 10 minutes | Serves 4

- 2 tablespoons extra-virgin olive oil or unrefined virgin coconut oil
- 1 teaspoon minced fresh ginger
- 1 cup peeled and finely diced Garnet sweet potato
- ⅛ teaspoon ground cinnamon
- ¼ cup Magic Mineral Broth or water
- 3 cups cleaned, stemmed, and chopped dinosaur kale, in bite-size pieces
- ¼ teaspoon sea salt
- 2 tablespoons golden raisins
- ¼ teaspoon maple syrup
- 2 tablespoons ground pecans, for garnish

1. Heat the oil in a large sauté pan over medium heat, then add the ginger and sauté for 30 seconds, just until aromatic.
2. Add the sweet potato, cinnamon, and broth and sauté for about 1 minute.
3. Add the kale, salt, and raisins and sauté until the kale is a darker shade of green and the sweet potatoes are tender, about 5 minutes.
4. Stir in the maple syrup, then taste; you might want to add another pinch of salt if desired.
5. Serve garnished with the ground pecans.

PER SERVING

Calories: 160 | Total Fat: 10.1g | Sat Fat: 1.3g | Carbohydrates: 17g | Protein: 3g | Fiber: 3g | Sodium: 200mg

Kale with Carrots

Prep time: 5 minutes | Cook time: 35 minutes | Serves 4

- 4 cups stemmed and chopped Tuscan kale, in bite-size pieces
- 2 tablespoons extra-virgin olive oil
- 1 red onion, cut into half moons
- Sea salt
- 2 carrots, peeled and diced small
- 3 cloves garlic, minced
- 1 teaspoon minced fresh ginger
- 2 tablespoons freshly squeezed lemon juice

1. Cover the kale with cold water and set aside.
2. Heat the olive oil in a large, deep sauté pan over medium-high heat, then add the onion and a pinch of salt and sauté for 3 minutes. Decrease the heat to low and cook slowly until the onions are caramelized, about 20 minutes.
3. Increase the heat to medium, add the carrots, garlic, ginger, and a pinch of salt, and sauté for 3 to 4 minutes, until the carrots are tender.
4. Drain the kale and add it to the pan along with a scant ¼ teaspoon of salt. Sauté until the greens turn bright green and wilt, about 3 minutes.
5. Test the greens; you may need to add 1 tablespoon of water and continue cooking, covered, until they become just a little more tender, 2 to 3 minutes.
6. Drizzle on the lemon juice and stir gently. Serve immediately.

PER SERVING

Calories: 120 | Total Fat: 7.6g | Sat Fat: 1.1g | Carbohydrates: 14g | Protein: 3g | Fiber: 3g | Sodium: 125mg

Broccoli with Garlic and Ginger

Prep time: 10 minutes | Cook time: 5 minutes | Serves 4

- ½ teaspoon sea salt
- 1 large bunch broccoli, cut into florets, stems peeled and cut into bite-size pieces
- 1 tablespoon extra-virgin olive oil or coconut oil
- 1 tablespoon grated ginger
- 2 garlic cloves, chopped

1. Bring a large pot of water to a boil. Add the salt. Add the broccoli and blanch for 30 seconds.
2. Drain the broccoli, then run it under cold water to stop the cooking process; this will retain its lush green color.
3. Heat the oil in a sauté pan over medium heat.
4. Add the ginger and garlic and sauté for 30 seconds, just until aromatic.
5. Stir in the broccoli and a pinch of salt and sauté for 2 minutes; the broccoli should still be firm. Serve immediately.

PER SERVING

Calories: 70 | Total Fat: 4g | Sat Fat: 0g | Carbohydrates: 6g | Protein: 2g | Fiber: 2g | Sodium: 323mg

Arugula with Edamame, Radish, and Avocado

Prep time: 15 minutes | Cook time: 10 minutes | Serves 4

- 6 cups arugula or mixed salad greens
- 1 cup fresh or frozen shelled edamame, mixed with a spritz of fresh lime juice and a pinch of sea salt
- 4 radishes, trimmed and sliced
- 1 avocado, spritzed with fresh lime juice and sprinkled with sea salt (so it doesn't discolor)
- ¼ cup Cilantro Lime Vinaigrette

1. Combine the arugula or mixed greens with the edamame, radishes, and avocado in a large bowl.
2. Add the vinaigrette and toss to combine before serving.

PER SERVING

Calories: 160 | Total Fat: 11.2g | Sat Fat: 1.4g | Carbohydrates: 12g | Protein: 5g | Fiber: 5g | Sodium: 200 mg

Warm and Toasty Cumin Carrots

Prep time: 10 minutes | Cook time: 5 minutes | Serves 4

- ½ teaspoon cumin seeds
- 2 tablespoons extra-virgin olive oil
- 1 teaspoon minced fresh ginger
- 1½ cups peeled and sliced carrots, cut ¼ inch thick
- ¼ teaspoon sea salt
- 2 tablespoons water
- 1 teaspoon freshly squeezed lemon juice
- 1 teaspoon maple syrup
- Chopped fresh parsley, for garnish

1. Toast the cumin seeds in a dry sauté pan over medium heat, shaking the pan back and forth until they start to pop and become aromatic.
2. Immediately add the olive oil and ginger and sauté for 1 minute.
3. Stir in the carrots and salt, then turn down the heat to medium-low, add the water, cover, and cook for about 2 minutes, until just barely tender.
4. Stir in the lemon juice and maple syrup. Garnish with the parsley and serve immediately.

PER SERVING

Calories: 85 | Total Fat: 7.2g | Sat Fat: 1g | Carbohydrates: 6g | Protein: 0g | Fiber: 1g | Sodium: 180mg

Mashed Cinnamon Butternut Squash

Prep time: 15 minutes | Cook time: 35 minutes | Serves 4

- 1 butternut squash, peeled and cut into 1-inch cubes, or one package of precut butternut squash
- 2 tablespoons extra-virgin olive oil
- ¼ teaspoon ground cinnamon
- ¼ teaspoon ground ginger, or 1 teaspoon grated fresh ginger
- Sea salt
- ¼ teaspoon maple syrup
- ⅛ teaspoon freshly grated nutmeg
- 1 teaspoon lemon juice (optional)

1. Preheat the oven to 400°F and line a baking sheet with parchment paper.
2. Toss the squash with the olive oil, cinnamon, ginger, and ¼ teaspoon of salt until the squash is well coated, then spread it in a single layer on the prepared pan.
3. Roast for 25 to 30 minutes, until soft and tender.
4. Transfer the squash to a food processor, add the maple syrup, nutmeg, and a pinch of salt, and process until smooth and creamy.
5. Taste. If you think it needs a little extra punch, try adding 1 teaspoon of fresh lemon juice.

PER SERVING

Calories: 160 | Total Fat: 7.2g | Sat Fat: 1.1g | Carbohydrates: 25g | Protein: 2 g | Fiber: 4g | Sodium: 155mg

Roasted Root Vegetables with Rosemary and Thyme

Prep time: 20 minutes | Cook time: 40 minutes | Serves 6

- 2 pounds root vegetables (such as potatoes, sweet potatoes, carrots, parsnips, turnips, rutabagas), peeled and cut into 1-inch cubes
- 2 tablespoons extra-virgin olive oil
- ½ teaspoon sea salt
- ½ teaspoon freshly ground pepper
- 1 tablespoon chopped fresh rosemary, or ¼ teaspoon dried
- 1½ tablespoons chopped fresh thyme, or ½ teaspoon dried
- 1 tablespoon freshly squeezed lemon or orange juice (optional)
- 2 tablespoons chopped fresh parsley, for garnish

1. Preheat the oven to 400°F and line a large baking sheet with parchment paper.
2. In a large bowl, toss the vegetables with the olive oil, salt, pepper, rosemary, and thyme until evenly coated.
3. Spread the vegetables in a single layer on the prepared pan (using two pans if need be).
4. Bake for 30 to 40 minutes, or until tender.
5. Transfer to a bowl or platter and spritz with the lemon juice, if desired, and sprinkle with the parsley. Serve immediately.

PER SERVING

Calories 130g | Total Fat: 3.7g | Sat Fat: 0.5g | Carbohydrates: 15.5g | Protein: 1.7g | Fiber: 4g | Sodium: 145mg

Stir-Fried Baby Bok Choy with Shiitake Mushrooms

Prep time: 15 minutes | Cook time: 5 minutes | Serves 6

- 4 heads baby bok choy
- 2 tablespoons light sesame oil
- 2 scallions, white parts only, thinly sliced
- 2 tablespoons minced fresh ginger
- 2 cloves garlic, minced
- ½ pound shiitake mushrooms, stemmed and sliced ¼ inch thick
- Sea salt
- 2 tablespoons water
- 1 tablespoon tamari
- 1 tablespoon freshly squeezed lime juice
- 1½ teaspoons toasted sesame oil
- 1 tablespoon toasted sesame seeds

1. Trim the bases off the bok choy and discard. Trim the leaves from the stems and cut both crosswise into bite-size pieces, keeping the stems and leaves separate.
2. Heat the light sesame oil in a sauté pan over medium heat, then add the scallions, ginger, garlic, mushrooms, and a pinch of salt and sauté for 30 seconds.
3. Add the water, tamari, and the bok choy stems and sauté for 2 minutes.
4. Add the bok choy leaves, lime juice, toasted sesame oil, and a pinch of salt and sauté until the bok choy is just wilted, about 2 minutes.
5. Taste and add another squeeze of lime if you like. Sprinkle with the toasted sesame seeds and serve immediately.

PER SERVING

Calories: 150 | Total Fat: 7.8g | Sat Fat: 1g | Carbohydrates: 16g | Protein: 10g | Fiber: 6g | Sodium: 585mg

Warm Napa Cabbage Slaw

Prep time: 10 minutes | Cook time: 10 minutes | Serves 4

- 2 tablespoons rice vinegar
- 2 tablespoons tamari
- 1 teaspoon maple syrup
- 1 tablespoon minced fresh ginger
- 1 tablespoon light sesame oil
- 1 cup thinly sliced red onion
- Sea salt
- 2 cups shredded napa cabbage
- 1 cup shredded red cabbage
- 1 cup peeled and shredded carrots
- ¼ cup fresh cilantro leaves

1. Whisk the vinegar, tamari, maple syrup, and ginger together in a bowl.
2. Heat the sesame oil in a large sauté pan over medium heat, then add the onion and a pinch of salt and sauté until the onion is translucent, about 3 minutes.
3. Add the napa cabbage, red cabbage, carrots, and a pinch of salt and sauté until the cabbage is slightly wilted, about 2 minutes.
4. Stir in the vinegar mixture and cook until the liquid is reduced by half and coats the vegetables. Remove from the heat and stir in the cilantro.

PER SERVING

Calories: 85 | Total Fat: 3.7g | Sat Fat: 0.5g | Carbohydrates: 11g | Protein: 2g | Fiber: 2g | Sodium: 610mg

Chapter 8
Fun Sides and Savory Snacks

Cancer'S Gone Crackers

Prep time: 20 minutes | Cool time: 12 hours | Dehydrate time: 15 to 20 hours | Serves 20

- 3 cups ground flaxseeds
- 1 cup sunflower seeds
- 2 tablespoons minced onion or 3 tablespoons onion powder
- 2 tablespoons sesame seeds
- 1 tablespoon minced garlic or 2 tablespoons garlic powder
- 2 teaspoons cumin powder
- 1 teaspoon chili powder
- 1 teaspoon sea salt
- 1 teaspoon cayenne pepper
- ½ teaspoon turmeric
- ½ cup filtered water

1. Put all the dry ingredients in the bowl of a food processor and blend until a fine, flourlike consistency is achieved.
2. Add the water and mix until a batter forms. Cover and allow the batter to set in the fridge for 12 hours.
3. Spread a ⅛-inch layer of batter on nonstick dehydrator sheets and dehydrate at 100°F for 15 to 20 hours. (Use a dehydrator kitchen appliance, or for an oven alternative see Tips below.)
4. Cut or break the cracker sheet into pieces the size of your choice and store in an airtight container at room temperature or in the fridge for up to 8 weeks.

PER SERVING

Calories: 138.7 | Protein: 4.8g | Carbs: 6.9g | Dietary Fiber: 5.4g | Fat: 11.2g | Vitamin C: 0.4mg | Vitamin D: 0 IU | Vitamin E: 2.6mg | Calcium: 61.7mg | Iron: 1.7mg | Magnesium: 92.4mg | Potassium: 200mg

Guacamole

Prep time: 5 minutes | Cook time: 10 minutes | Serves 1

- 1 avocado
- ¼ teaspoon sea salt
- ¼ teaspoon black pepper
- Juice of ½ lemon

1. Mash the avocado in a bowl with a fork.
2. Blend in the other ingredients.

PER SERVING

Calories: 328 | Protein: 4.1g | Carbs: 19g | Dietary Fiber: 13.6g | Fat: 29.5g | Vitamin C: 28.9mg | Vitamin D: 0 IU | Vitamin E: 4.2mg | Calcium: 28mg | Iron: 1.1mg | Magnesium: 60.6mg | Potassium: 1,006mg

Gluten-Free Tortillas

Prep time: 5 minutes | Cook time: 20 minutes | Serves 6

- 1 ½ cups rice flour
- ½ cup tigernut flour
- 1 cups buckwheat flour
- 1 cup warm filtered water
- 2 teaspoons apple cider vinegar
- 1 tablespoon Flax Egg Alternative

1. Combine the rice, tigernut, and buckwheat flours in a large bowl. Slowly add the water and vinegar, stirring constantly to combine. Add the Flax Egg Alternative, mixing well to form the dough.
2. Knead the dough for 2 minutes until it feels tougher and form into a ball.
3. Roll out the ball of dough with a rolling pin to make six 6-inch circles (⅙ cup of dough each).
4. Heat a cast-iron pan on the stove over medium heat. Place the dough circles in the hot pan. Cover the pan while the dough cooks. (This is important for the softness of the tortillas.) Cook for 1 to 2 minutes on each side until there is no more soft dough.
5. Once the tortillas are ready, transfer them to a plate and cover with a clean dish towel or cotton napkin to keep them soft. They are best eaten the day they're made.

PER SERVING

Calories: 248.8 | Protein: 6.8g | Carbs: 51.8g | Dietary Fiber: 5.1g | Fat: 2.3g | Vitamin C: 0mg | Vitamin D: 0 IU | Vitamin E: 0.3mg | Calcium: 20.1mg | Iron: 2mg | Magnesium: 119.9mg | Potassium: 288.4mg

Coconut Wraps

Prep time: 15 minutes | Dehydrate time: 16 hours | Serves 2

- 2 cups raw coconut meat (from young coconuts or green coconuts), about 4 to 6 coconuts
- 1 tablespoon coconut water (when you open the coconut)
- ¼ teaspoon sea salt

1. Add the coconut meat, coconut water, and sea salt to a food processor and process until the mixture is completely smooth.
2. If it is too dry, add more coconut water, up to another tablespoon.
3. Spread the coconut batter to ¼-inch thickness on a dehydrator sheet (or baking paper).
4. Dehydrate the batter at 105°F for 8 to 9 hours. At the 8-hour mark the top will be dry and solid. Turn the batter over and dehydrate for another 8 to 9 hours.

PER SERVING

Calories: 284.6 | Protein: 2.7g | Carbs: 12.4g | Dietary Fiber: 7.2g | Fat: 26.8g | Vitamin C: 2.8mg | Vitamin D: 0 IU | Vitamin E: 0.1mg | Calcium: 13mg | Iron: 1.9mg | Magnesium: 27.4mg | Potassium: 303.5mg

Stuffed Olives

Prep time: 10 minutes | Cook time: 10 minutes | Serves 4

- 2 cups fresh olives, pitted
- 1 red pepper, diced

1. Place the olives on a sheet or plate and simply insert a piece of pepper inside each olive.

PER SERVING

Calories: 74.9 | Protein: 0.8g | Carbs: 1.7g | Dietary Fiber: 0.6g | Fat: 7.1g | Vitamin C: 37.9mg | Vitamin D: 0 IU | Vitamin E: 1.7mg | Calcium: 40.9mg | Iron: 0.7mg | Magnesium: 17.6mg | Potassium: 120.8mg

Turmeric Hummus

Prep time: 10 minutes| Cook time: 10 minutes | Serves 4

- One 14-ounce can chickpeas
- ¼ cup aquafaba (water from the can of chickpeas)
- 2 tablespoons garlic salt
- 1 ½ tablespoons lemon juice
- 1 ½ tablespoons sesame seeds
- 1 ½ tablespoons turmeric powder
- 1 tablespoon sesame seed oil
- 1 tablespoon flax oil, extra-virgin olive oil, or tigernut oil
- ½ teaspoon sea salt

1. Combine all ingredients in a food processor and process until smooth.

PER SERVING

Calories: 194.1 | Protein: 6.2g | Carbs: 21.9g | Dietary Fiber: 5.4g | Fat: 10.3g | Vitamin C: 2.3mg | Vitamin D: 0 IU | Vitamin E: 0.3mg | Calcium: 69.5mg | Iron: 2.8mg | Magnesium: 36.1mg | Potassium: 197.8mg

Chickpea Fries

Prep time: 10 minutes | Cook time: 10 minutes | Serves 1 to 2

- 1 tablespoon extra-virgin olive oil
- One 14-ounce can organic chickpeas, drained of liquid
- ¼ teaspoon sea salt
- Pepper, to taste

1. Heat a fry pan with oil over medium heat. When hot, add the chickpeas.
2. Sprinkle with salt and pepper, then cook for 5 to 7 minutes or until the chickpeas are golden brown on the outside.

PER SERVING

Calories: 238.2 | Protein: 8.9g | Carbs: 29g | Dietary Fiber: 8g | Fat: 10.1g | Vitamin C: 0.1mg | Vitamin D: 0 IU | Vitamin E: 1.2mg | Calcium: 54.6mg | Iron: 1.2mg | Magnesium: 30.4mg | Potassium: 138.4mg

Hummus-Stuffed Peppers

Prep time: 10 minutes | Cook time: 10 minutes | Serves 1

- 1 bell pepper, any color
- ¾ cup Turmeric Hummus
- Paprika or cayenne pepper, to taste

1. Cut the bell pepper in half and scoop out the seeds.
2. Stuff each pepper half with hummus. Sprinkle with fresh spices like paprika and cayenne pepper.

PER SERVING

Calories: 615 | Protein: 20g | Carbs: 71g | Dietary Fiber: 18.9g | Fat: 31.9g | Vitamin C: 138.9mg | Vitamin D: 0 IU | Vitamin E: 1.6mg | Calcium: 224.9mg | Iron: 9mg | Magnesium: 124.8mg | Potassium: 880.5mg

Teff Crepes

Prep time: 10 minutes | **Set time:** 30 minutes | **Cook time:** 16 minutes | **Serves 8**

- 1 cup teff flour
- 1 cup almond milk (Note: If the almond milk has vanilla in it, the result will taste more like a dessert crepe.)
- ¼ cup filtered water
- 3 eggs
- 2 tablespoons olive oil, MCT oil, or coconut oil
- ¼ teaspoon sea salt
- Coconut oil, for frying

1. Add all the ingredients to a blender and mix until smooth and well combined. Let the batter sit for at least 30 minutes, or set in the fridge overnight.
2. Add ½ teaspoon coconut oil to a fry pan. When the oil is hot and melted over the entire surface of the pan, pour in the batter.
3. Cook, one crepe at a time, for 2 minutes or until the batter starts to bubble, then turn over. Cook for another 2 minutes, then serve.

PER SERVING

Calories: 167.7 | Protein: 5.8g | Carbs: 15.6g | Dietary Fiber: 3g | Fat: 9.2g | Vitamin C: 0mg | Vitamin D: 15.3 IU | Vitamin E: 0.6mg | Calcium: 53.6mg | Iron: 1.8mg | Magnesium: 14.6mg | Potassium: 58.7mg

Hard Vegan Cheese

Prep time: 15 minutes with overnight soaking | **Cool time:** 1 hour | **Serves 4**

- ¾ cup cashews
- 1 ½ teaspoon agar powder
- 1 cup filtered water, divided
- 1 tablespoon nutritional yeast
- 1 garlic clove
- 1 ½ teaspoons arrowroot flour or tapioca flour
- ⅛ teaspoon sea salt
- 2 tablespoons plus 1 teaspoon lemon juice
- ¼ teaspoon turmeric powder

1. Soak the cashews in filtered water overnight.
2. Mix the agar with ½ cup of filtered water in a saucepan. Do not apply heat yet; set aside.
3. Drain the cashews, then add them to a food processer with the nutritional yeast, garlic, arrowroot, sea salt, lemon juice, turmeric, and the remaining ½ cup of filtered water. Blend until the mixture is very smooth.
4. Add the cashew cheese to the agar pot and bring to a boil over low heat until it forms a thick batter consistency.
5. Transfer the mixture to a dish that you want the shape of your cheese to be in. You could divide it into cupcake holders, for example. Refrigerate the cheese for 1 hour and then enjoy.

PER SERVING

Calories: 148.7 | Protein: 5.1g | Carbs: 10.2g | Dietary Fiber: 1.1g | Fat: 10.7g | Vitamin C: 3.8mg | Vitamin D: 0 IU | Vitamin E: 0.2mg | Calcium: 18.7mg | Iron: 2mg | Magnesium: 74.2mg | Potassium: 203.9mg

Probiotic Pickled Cucumbers

Prep time: 5 minutes | Ferment time: 3–5 days | Serves 5

- 5 cucumbers
- 2 teaspoons mustard seeds
- 1 tablespoon dill
- 1 tablespoon sea salt
- 1 cup filtered water, room temperature

1. Place 5 whole cucumbers in a quart-size jar. Add the remaining ingredients. The water should cover the cucumbers completely, and the top of the liquid should be at least ½ inch below the top of the jar.
2. Cover tightly and store at room temperature for 3 to 5 days before refrigerating. The pickles will keep indefinitely.
3. Serve with salads and meat meals, or mix into stir-fries!

PER SERVING

Calories: 65 | Protein: 2.8g | Carbs: 14g | Dietary Fiber: 2g | Fat: 1g | Vitamin C: 10.7mg | Vitamin D: 0 IU | Vitamin E: 0.2mg | Calcium: 66.7mg | Iron: 1.2mg | Magnesium: 55.7mg | Potassium: 566.4mg

Simple Steamed Artichokes

Prep time: 10 minutes | Cook time: 40 minutes | Serves 3

- 1 lemon
- 2 teaspoons sea salt
- 3 whole artichokes

1. Fill a large pot ¾ full of water, adding the juice of 1 lemon and 2 teaspoons salt. Bring to a boil.
2. Place the artichokes in a steamer tray inside the pot, stem side up. Cover the pot and steam the artichokes until the hearts are tender and the inner leaves pull out easily. This will take about 25 to 35 minutes.
3. Remove the artichokes from the heat and serve.

PER SERVING

Calories: 79.5 | Protein: 5.3g | Carbs: 18g | Dietary Fiber: 8.7g | Fat: 0.2g | Vitamin C: 24.8mg | Vitamin D: 0 IU | Vitamin E: 0.3mg | Calcium: 72.1mg | Iron: 2mg | Magnesium: 98.1mg | Potassium: 615.1mg

Cashew Cheese

Prep time: 10 minutes | Cook time: 10 minutes | Serves 1

- 2 cups cashews
- 2 tablespoons nutritional yeast
- Juice of 1 small lemon (but no more than ¼ cup)
- ½ teaspoon sea salt
- ½ cup filtered water (more for a softer cheese)

1. Put all the ingredients in a food processor.
2. Blend until the mixture is smooth, adding more water if a softer cheese is desired.

PER SERVING

Calories: 369.5 | Protein: 12.8g | Carbs: 21g | Dietary Fiber: 2.5g | Fat: 28.6g | Vitamin C: 4.7mg | Vitamin D: 0 IU | Vitamin E: 0.6mg | Calcium: 26.4mg | Iron: 4.4mg | Magnesium: 193.7mg | Potassium: 474.1mg

Baked Kale Chips

Prep time: 10 minutes | Cook time: 10 minutes | Serves 2

- 1 packet or bunch of prewashed, precut kale
- 1 tablespoon extra-virgin olive oil
- 1 teaspoon sea salt

1. Preheat the oven to 400°F. Line a baking sheet with parchment paper. Lining with paper instead of oil will ensure faster bake time.
2. Add the kale to a bowl along with the oil and sea salt and massage until the leaves are well covered.
3. Bake for 9 minutes or until the edges of the kale are brown and crisp. They will dry out given time to rest after baking. Store in a dry place if you don't eat them all at once!

PER SERVING

Calories: 78.6 | Protein: 1.3g | Carbs: 2.8g | Dietary Fiber: 1.1g | Fat: 7.3g | Vitamin C: 38.4mg | Vitamin D: 0 IU | Vitamin E: 1.3mg | Calcium: 48mg | Iron: 0.4mg | Magnesium: 15mg | Potassium: 157.1mg

Appendix 1 Measurement Conversion Chart

Volume Equivalents (Dry)	
US STANDARD	METRIC (APPROXIMATE)
1/8 teaspoon	0.5 mL
1/4 teaspoon	1 mL
1/2 teaspoon	2 mL
3/4 teaspoon	4 mL
1 teaspoon	5 mL
1 tablespoon	15 mL
1/4 cup	59 mL
1/2 cup	118 mL
3/4 cup	177 mL
1 cup	235 mL
2 cups	475 mL
3 cups	700 mL
4 cups	1 L

Volume Equivalents (Liquid)		
US STANDARD	US STANDARD (OUNCES)	METRIC (APPROXIMATE)
2 tablespoons	1 fl.oz.	30 mL
1/4 cup	2 fl.oz.	60 mL
1/2 cup	4 fl.oz.	120 mL
1 cup	8 fl.oz.	240 mL
1 1/2 cup	12 fl.oz.	355 mL
2 cups or 1 pint	16 fl.oz.	475 mL
4 cups or 1 quart	32 fl.oz.	1 L
1 gallon	128 fl.oz.	4 L

Temperatures Equivalents	
FAHRENHEIT(F)	CELSIUS(C) APPROXIMATE)
225 °F	107 °C
250 °F	120 ° °C
275 °F	135 °C
300 °F	150 °C
325 °F	160 °C
350 °F	180 °C
375 °F	190 °C
400 °F	205 °C
425 °F	220 °C
450 °F	235 °C
475 °F	245 °C
500 °F	260 °C

Weight Equivalents	
US STANDARD	METRIC (APPROXIMATE)
1 ounce	28 g
2 ounces	57 g
5 ounces	142 g
10 ounces	284 g
15 ounces	425 g
16 ounces (1 pound)	455 g
1.5 pounds	680 g
2 pounds	907 g

Appendix 2 The Dirty Dozen and Clean Fifteen

The Environmental Working Group (EWG) is a nonprofit, nonpartisan organization dedicated to protecting human health and the environment Its mission is to empower people to live healthier lives in a healthier environment. This organization publishes an annual list of the twelve kinds of produce, in sequence, that have the highest amount of pesticide residue-the Dirty Dozen-as well as a list of the fifteen kinds ofproduce that have the least amount of pesticide residue-the Clean Fifteen.

THE DIRTY DOZEN	
The 2016 Dirty Dozen includes the following produce. These are considered among the year's most important produce to buy organic:	
Strawberries	Spinach
Apples	Tomatoes
Nectarines	Bell peppers
Peaches	Cherry tomatoes
Celery	Cucumbers
Grapes	Kale/collard greens
Cherries	Hot peppers

The Dirty Dozen list contains two additional itemskale/collard greens and hot peppers-because they tend to contain trace levels of highly hazardous pesticides.

THE CLEAN FIFTEEN	
The least critical to buy organically are the Clean Fifteen list. The following are on the 2016 list:	
Avocados	Papayas
Corn	Kiw
Pineapples	Eggplant
Cabbage	Honeydew
Sweet peas	Grapefruit
Onions	Cantaloupe
Asparagus	Cauliflower
Mangos	

Some of the sweet corn sold in the United States are made from genetically engineered (GE) seedstock. Buy organic varieties of these crops to avoid GE produce.

Appendix 3 Index

DINA S. ROY

Printed in the USA
CPSIA information can be obtained
at www.ICGtesting.com
LVHW072357031223
765556LV00042B/16

9 781805 380719